LEGACY

LEGACY

DAVID C. MARTIN AT AC MARTIN

WORKS FROM 1966 – 2016

DEDICATION

To my wife, Mary Klaus Martin, my children, Lee and Melanie, and my extended family of professional associates at AC Martin. All have contributed to the legacy, and I am grateful. — DCM

TABLE OF CONTENTS

Foreword	12	**Unbuilt Work**	196
David C. Martin	14	Oregon State University Student Center	198
		San Joaquin County Administration Building	199
A Way of Thinking	20	LAX Consolidated Rent-A-Car (ConRAC) Facility	200
		Temecula Resort and Spa	202
Built Work	26	Bakersfield Federal Courthouse	203
		Ventura History Museum	204

Wilshire Grand Center — 28
Madera County Courthouse — 52
Fresno State Library — 68
Chapman University Interfaith Center — 78
Hollenbeck Community Police Station — 92
Fifth District Court of Appeal — 102
UC Irvine Humanities/Music/Fine Arts Buildings — 110
Caltrans District 3 Headquarters — 116
UC Davis Mathematical Sciences Building — 124
CalEPA Headquarters — 128
Springleaf Tower — 136
USC Ronald Tutor Campus Center — 140
Flintridge Prep Performing Arts Center — 150
Rustic Canyon Residence — 156
Padre Serra Parish — 174

LAUSD 17th and Grand High School — 206
Mattel Design Center — 207
Chapman University Anaconda Student Housing — 208
Central California History Museum — 210
Grand Avenue Development — 212
Towers — 214

Furniture Design — 218

Project Chronology — 234

Acknowledgments — 244

Christopher C. Martin — 245
AC Martin Staff and Clients — 246

Credits — 248

Contributors to *Legacy* — 249
Photographers — 249

Inspiration — 178

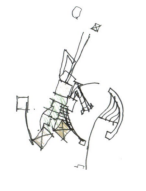

FOREWORD

In 1904, a young Albert C. Martin moved from the Midwest to Los Angeles. The city had a booming population and was rapidly growing into a mecca of industry, production, and manufacturing. Hollywood was becoming the film capital of the world. It was a city on the verge of cultural explosion, a city of dreams — the place for Albert to realize *his* dream.

By 1906, he had pulled together enough savings to open his architectural firm, Albert C. Martin & Associates. The firm still stands and thrives, having produced in its history some of the most famous works in Los Angeles, including St. Vincent de Paul Church (1925), L.A. City Hall (1928), May Company at Lakewood Center (1952), L.A. Department of Water and Power/John Ferraro Building (1965), St. Basil Roman Catholic Church (1969), Figueroa at Wilshire, a 50-story office building (1990), and Wilshire Grand Center, a 75-story hotel and office building (2017). An L.A. Times article in 1979 credited the firm with designing over half of the downtown skyline since WWII. There is a presence to the name AC Martin that carries weight within Los Angeles, as both have flourished together.

The firm remained a family business through three generations. Albert's sons—Albert, Jr. and J. Edward—represented the second generation. Albert's grandsons—David C. Martin, design principal from 1984–2016, and Christopher C. Martin, named managing partner in 1986—represented the third generation. Chris later served as chairman and CEO through 2019, and he remains chairman today. The firm's fourth generation continues as a partnership of talent leaders dedicated to the same values of business integrity and attention to craft that Albert instilled in the practice over a century ago.

While his built projects for AC Martin may be the most public aspect of his life's work, David Martin has always maintained deep ties with the design community in L.A. and beyond, spearheading innovation and creativity and mentoring students who represent the future of design. In 2005, David was invited by his alma mater, USC, to create a furniture design studio in the School of Architecture. It remains one of the school's most popular courses. He co-founded the design think-tank and incubator Martin Architecture and Design Workshop (MADWORKSHOP) with his wife, Mary, in 2015.

As a third-generation architect, David learned valuable lessons from his father and grandfather and countless lessons of his own over his 50-year career. He is sharing this knowledge with today's young designers, and they are sharing their unique perspectives with him in return. David participates in this creative discourse to push design in new directions. It is his way of carrying on the legacy.

Albert C. Martin, Jr., Albert C. Martin, Sr., J. Edward Martin

J. Edward Martin, Christopher C. Martin, David C. Martin, Albert C. Martin, Jr.

Christopher C. Martin, David C. Martin

DAVID C. MARTIN
Edie Cohen

David C. Martin is steeped in both the history and culture of Los Angeles. Though he identifies as an architect and Angeleno, he is so much more. First, he is a citizen of the world. His travels blend study and learning with pure pleasure. At 15, his first trip to Europe introduced him to piazzas and cities created for pedestrians and public transportation, sparking a life-long fascination with city planning. Always with a camera and sketchbook in hand, he used film and watercolor as his means of expression, his memories, and his diaries. Still today, he delights in watercolor. It is the language with which he memorializes places and experiences, explores concepts, and solves design problems of all scales. So David is an artist too.

He is also a builder and maker. Being encouraged as a teenager to construct a car for himself sparked his life-long love of automotive design. This has come to fruition with David seeing Europe from a new vantage point: the driver's seat of an Alfa Romeo Touring Spider in Italy's famed Mille Miglia, as well as from his hand-built hot rod for the Bernina Gran Turismo race, taking him through the hairpin turns of the Swiss Alps.

Designing his Rustic Canyon residence that he shares with Mary, David was introduced to design's grande dame, Andrée Putman, who selected the home's furnishings. From this friendship arose a fascination with and desire to create furnishings of his own. David embraced the maker movement, designing and fabricating seating and lighting fixtures in his on-site workshop.

To pay this enthusiasm forward, David launched a furniture design course at USC, guiding students across disciplines to design and construct a piece, critiqued by an outside panel of professionals. This engagement with students was the genesis of the Martin's MADWORKSHOP Foundation. MADWORKSHOP creates space and opportunity for students, artists, and designers in the fields of architecture, furniture design, product design, fashion, art, and robotics to learn and test new skills and ideas.

MADWORKSHOP partners with prestigious design schools such as USC, Pratt Institute, Art Center College of Design, UCLA, and Otis College of Art and Design, and sponsors international artistic installations, including the Venice Biennale. The goal is to elevate the next generation of design thinkers and craftspeople who will carry on the work to grow and shape not only the City of L.A., but the world.

There's no doubt that David is a true Renaissance man. He's an architect and designer, artist, builder, and educator. He's also a musician, playing jazz guitar. Surprisingly, he has an avid interest in fashion as well. He and Mary can often be seen seated among the first few rows of haute couture shows for Chanel, Gucci, Fendi, and Jason Wu. "I'm interested in the design of absolutely everything," David says.

Looking to the future, David envisions much more travel and MADWORKSHOP's expanded endeavors to be major focal points of his life. As a patron of the American Academy in Rome, he is planning for increased involvement in Italy. One objective is a sponsored competition on urban design. In Varese, home to Via Sacra, leading past 14 frescoed chapels, David and members of the Foundation will oversee an artistic performance. And in Casciago, he is planning to transform a decommissioned church into a cultural center. Closer to home, David is focusing on improving architecture and design education, particularly addressing diversity and inclusion at the high school and college levels.

We recently sat down together for a Q&A session about his career path, his passions, key motivators, and industry challenges.

Given AC Martin's legacy, how did you take over the family business? Did you start off intimidated by following in your father's and grandfather's footsteps?

It was clear to me that I'd be an architect. My mom realized that I had something. I was creative. I could draw. At a young age, I was singled out as *the chosen one,* so I knew this was my destiny and didn't fight it. I joined the family business. As the boss's son, people both criticize and fear you, but that never bothered me. I liked it.

My father was in partnership with his brother, Ed. Ed's son, Chris, was the chosen one on his side of the family. The frightening thing during our early partnership was whether Chris and I could keep the machine going, but there was a moment when we realized the third generation would be successful; one reason being we both had clear roles. Chris was the businessman, and I was the artist. We generally stayed on our own turf. We did good work. I'm very proud of it.

What makes a good architect and designer?

If we would step away and look at other professions, such as filmmaker or dot-com guy, I'd say the same ingredients apply. You have to be optimistic and have imagination. You have to keep your priorities straight and have an internal belief that your clients want the project to be inspiring, imaginative, have a spirit, and be a good place to work. You have to believe that you can deliver on that and know there will be obstacles.

I'm inspired by delivering and finding a balance between creativity and functionality. It's better to err on the side of creativity, but you still have to produce a functioning project. There have been comparisons to architecture and the right brain/left brain separation. Can an architect deliver on both the creative talent and business sides of the profession? Are both necessary? Yeah, and history is full of examples.

I want to make another point. There are a lot of comparable fields in which you have to be inventive and have a dialogue between business and creativity: medicine, science, and aerospace, to name a few. A great doctor, for instance, is not going to run a hospital but will do research. Cinema is a classic example, with the producer, director, and film star all in divided roles to create the goods. Great architecture is usually a product of such a system. It takes more than one person.

Who has inspired you?

Frank Lloyd Wright, Carlo Scarpa, Richard Neutra, and Le Corbusier. It was great knowing John Lautner. Renzo Piano is one of my favorites, as is David Chipperfield. Frank Gehry is probably one of the most famous architects in the world. The Vuitton Foundation in Paris is incredible—the best he's done.

One of the great firms is SOM, as was Adler & Sullivan. I see furniture design as an extension of architecture, so I must include Eileen Gray, Pierre Chareau, and Jean-Michel Frank on this list.

And not only the design masters have inspired me. An important part of my life has been learning about architecture built around a communal society where architecture and community reinforce each other. Think of Italian towns where everything important faces a central piazza. This can also be seen in India, in Persia, and in the Maya Region. I learned this through osmosis via traveling.

The best advice you've been given? Advice you'd give those entering the profession?

All those stupid proverbs my mother told me wound up being true. "You can catch more flies with honey than with vinegar" was one of her favorites.

The advice I give to kids: It's important to have a master's degree. It's important to live somewhere else and travel — how can one study great public spaces without being part of them? Architecture is not style or a single layer. It has depth, proportionality, materiality, color, form, and yes, engineering.

How did your passion for watercolor come about? Did it come easily, or did you struggle?

I went to boarding school at 15. There was no art education whatsoever there. My mom insisted I have art lessons, and I loved them. I started to paint cars, castles, and airplanes. Years later, I got together with architects, landscape architects, and artists. We traveled the world together and painted. Easy? It's still hard. I'm not a natural, but I work at it.

LA CIENEGA   2/12/14   PCM

What are your greatest talents/greatest defects?

My greatest talent? I could get interested in the workings of anything. I have a genuine curiosity that I've had since I was a little boy, fascinated by my imagination. Mary has the same fascination. I love the design process. It carries over into music, art, architecture, and fashion. Maybe my defect is I don't need to win, but I do need to be in the game. When you're always in the game, sometimes you win.

Cite two projects at opposite ends of the scale spectrum of which you are particularly proud.

The obvious ones are the Wilshire Grand and the little chapel at Chapman University. Both are my favorites because I was allowed to breathe, so to speak. Wilshire Grand was big and technical. It had the thrill of engineering and pushing the limits of computers and structural systems, understanding wind loads, types of glass, energy efficiency, natural ventilation, and air circulation. The challenge with the chapel was to create a spiritual space and deal with something as fundamental as religion without using icons. We could use more places for quiet contemplation to counter the din of the entertainment venues ubiquitous in today's society.

Speaking of challenges, what are the challenges in the architectural profession now and in the near future?

Architecture has shifted. Every few years, emphasis is placed on new and different aspects of architecture.

With the civil rights movement, the focus was on designing buildings that were welcoming to all, which opened up and enriched the profession. Then came sustainability and the need to use less energy. Focus then moved to accessibility, with laws established to make it a primary criterion for architects.

None of these considerations go away.

The challenge is that a building will last for more than 100 years and will have to weather these shifts in culture, society, and technology, but solely following trends can lead to problems. Since we only have five years to educate a student, we must offer a broad-based curriculum, balancing the study of these important, emergent issues with timeless fundamentals.

We can't be set in our ways.

How do you envision the profession morphing?

For sure, you have to be a digital native. You have to be able to communicate, convince people, and be a craftsman. Everyone must be fast on one's feet. The younger generation is growing up this way.

If you hadn't been an architect?

I would have been an automobile designer, a product designer, or a graphic artist; never a doctor, lawyer, or businessman. I wouldn't have had the interest.

A WAY OF THINKING

AC Martin has been in practice for over 118 years. Was there a philosophy that drove its success for three generations? For the second and third generations, it was the tenets of modernism, particularly related to Southern California in the post-war period. In the '50s, as the firm developed strength and grew, new materials, open space, aerospace, and inventive infrastructure accomplishments in our region led to an attitude of incredible optimism about cities and our future. Simplicity, economy of means, form, function, durability, and a fascination with technology informed our design solutions.

But within our firm, there was something more. If you look at the personal lifestyles of the second and third-generation partners—my father, Al, my uncle, Ed, my cousin, Chris, and me—all of us were builders. It was this common characteristic that gave the firm a reverence for craft and its many lessons. My father built and raced sailboats. He was also an excellent furniture builder. In fact, growing up, a workshop was located next to our family room. If my siblings or I wanted some material object, we were encouraged to make use of the workshop and build it ourselves. From this upbringing, I became a car builder and racer and also a furniture maker, designer, and teacher. Chris is a builder and technician. He once built and flew his own plane. Ed was an engineer, car enthusiast, and admirer of all things technical. Putting materials together well, seeing the beauty in detail, emphasizing functionality, and striving for exceptional levels of craftsmanship; this was how we all lived our lives. There was never any discussion about doing things other than the right way. Craftsmanship was mutually exciting to all of us.

As I matured in my architectural experiences and education, I quickly realized how important it was for modernist principles to evolve. Buildings needed to fit into (or establish) context to benefit their occupants. In turn, the architecture needed to embody a larger social responsibility to the community at large.

This sensibility started early for me. I grew up in a beautiful modern house my father had designed. It had an open plan, gorgeous furniture, and the latest materials and systems.

On my eighth birthday, I was taken to the Frank Lloyd Wright-designed V.C. Morris Gift Store on Maiden Lane in San Francisco. I immediately knew this was different from the architecture I was accustomed to. Its small, arched entry led into this fantastical, spirally space. The building defined space in a way I had not seen before. This was not an open plan, but instead, a space that wrapped around all of its contents and occupants. I loved it. It was memorable. And I found myself returning there again and again.

As I grew a bit older, I traveled to Europe and experienced the classic medieval plazas that formed the heart and soul of its cities. This was another new and fabulous experience for me. These spaces felt like a scaled-up version of the Morris Store. The architecture wrapped around to create a community gathering place, specifically designed to encourage the community to congregate for elemental reasons: protection, communication, security, food, and water.

Modernist principles did not address any of this.

I remember a day in one of my studio classes at USC. I asked my professor, Craig Elwood, about the excitement of the European plazas. He responded that although they were important in the history of architecture, they had nothing to do with what we were doing in our class. We were doing something entirely different.

That was the attitude in the '50s and '60s and often up to the present day. Buildings became islands in terms of context. They were functional, beautiful, and embodied their own set of rules, and were critiqued as isolated objects.

Rustic Canyon Residence

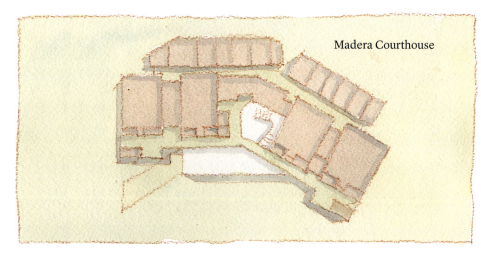
Madera Courthouse

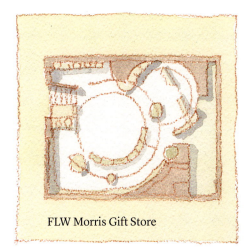
FLW Morris Gift Store

Chapman Chapel

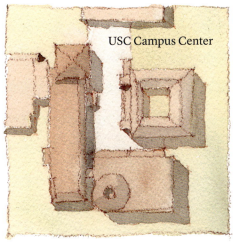
USC Campus Center

CALEPA Headquaters

Open Space Diagrams

Problems arose with modernism when these isolated buildings started to crowd existing, organized, contextual environments like university campuses and mature cities. These modernist growth spurts of the '40s and '50s tore apart the traditional master plans and created chaotic places and spaces. Local examples that come to mind are the campuses of Caltech, UCLA, and USC, in addition to most urban redevelopment areas in our established cities.

In 1967, while pursuing a master's degree at Columbia University, a new urban design attitude was forming. Our heroes were Jane Jacobs (author of *The Death and Life of Great American Cities*), William H. Whyte (*The Social Life of Small Urban Spaces*), and Christopher Alexander (*A New Theory of Urban Design*). I received a fellowship to study significant urban spaces in Italy, Spain, India, Morocco, Egypt, and Iran. By the '70s, I had my first opportunities to draw upon these earlier travels and observations as a designer at AC Martin. This way of thinking about urban design helped me realize that, as a firm, we could affect what happened within the walls of architecture, as well as outside, in the more public spaces.

Corporations were becoming educated on efficiency and the concept that esprit de corps could be encouraged through environmental design. Similarly, universities started talking about collegiality or positive communication between faculty, students, and the outside world (e.g., "town and gown"). As we collaborated and learned from each other, I realized we could improve communication and boost social interaction through the careful arrangement of stairs, halls, restrooms, drinking fountains, and coffee rooms. The joy of community was demonstrably enhanced by placing targeted emphasis on these spaces and functions in our design solutions.

Believe me. This was not on the modernist agenda.

Here are a few examples of what we learned from pursuing these ideas:

Indoor Communal Spaces

Within buildings, creating central spaces which most all occupants would pass through would generate chance meetings, sharing of work, educational experiences, and brainstorming. If you accommodated chance meetings with appropriate furnishings and media, an even more positive community interface would occur. There were always exceptions, but these moves typically worked. Looking back at historic and indigenous architecture, it's apparent that the more organic prototypes for community space—courtyards, atriums, and cloisters—all had specific social functions.

Outdoor Communal Spaces

Choreographing external space was more challenging as it either entailed interacting with new construction or proposing new landscape ideas. Here, we were often trying to use or activate space that was often referred to as "leftover." Inspired by William H. Whyte, we developed a series of ingredients. Active public spaces almost always had the following: both sun and shade, places to sit, some form of landscape, and available food and/or drink. Public spaces also served as some form of path or crossroad. Recovering and activating this public space led to more efficient space utilization. At the same time, we created a dialogue between the indoor and outdoor spaces of the project.

Common Spaces Within the Urban Fabric

In urban areas, the sidewalk was critical to livable cities. How a building reacted to the pedestrian circulation of a city was important to good design. Again, openings, architectural details, landscape, inviting entryways — all were moves beyond an empty plaza in front of a set-back office block, and all were something to aspire to. Christopher Alexander, in *A New Theory of Urban Design*, pointed out that every building needs to be a proper citizen but must also make its neighbors look good. In the '70s and '80s, a new language called for wide, pleasant sidewalks with solar access, creating significant and enjoyable open spaces.

Michael Heizer
North, East, South, West, 1981
Citigroup Center
444 S. Flower Street
Los Angeles, CA

These were the concerns of the pedestrian experience and street landscape. Granted, these were desirable traits for earlier modernist buildings, but at the time, corporate impressions of majesty and power were more important than creating dignified public environments.

Processional Spaces

We designed several religious spaces. We realized that thinking about the religious experience as a journey from a material world to a spiritual world made sense. Creating a procession of architectural spaces could reinforce the religious experience. Courtyard—to pergola—to entry—to intimate corridor—into grand dramatic space with chapels and art and vistas controlled along the journey—would create a timeless narrative. It was important to create spaces unlike what we would experience in the outside world. In other words, our thinking focused more on procession than religious ritual.

Art

The combination of art and architecture is a significant part of many great public spaces. Think of Piazza Navona in Rome (Bernini and Borromini), and Rockefeller Plaza in New York (Raymond Hood, Wallace Harrison, Diego Rivera, Isamu Noguchi, Lee Lawrie, Gaston Lachaise, and others.) Contemporary examples include some of our more enlightened federal buildings or the best of our elegant corporate architecture.

As a third-generation architect, I inherited the notion of working with artists to help create meaningful public spaces. My grandfather's buildings were often rich with figurative work, usually depicting themes of the original purpose of the building. In his design for the Ventura County Courthouse (1913), the mannerist architectural orders were sprinkled with statues of monks depicting the romanticized mission life, its models being workmen from the Gladding McBean terra cotta company.

In Sid Grauman's Million Dollar Theater on Broadway in downtown L.A. (1917), long-horn cattle and cowboy figures dominate the motif. For St. Vincent de Paul Catholic Church at the corner of Figueroa and West Adams in downtown L.A. (1925), a family came from Italy to carve the figures of saints for the major façade. To complete their work, they lived in a camp on the construction site for several months.

My father personally introduced me to the artists Alexander Calder, Claire Falkenstein, Isamu Noguchi, and Bauhaus artist Herbert Bayer, among others. This artist interaction was a natural extension of AC Martin's high-end corporate and religious commissions.

My interest in art grew out of these experiences. Mary and I became part of the L.A. art scene at very young ages, and working with artists became a natural part of a number of our commissions. One of the first for me was an office building in L.A. for the Rockefeller Family Trust. The cast of artists was stellar: Michael Heizer, Mark di Suvero, Robert Rauschenberg, Frank Stella, and Bruce Nauman. The excitement of the process and the end result were significant. From there, it continued with Eric Orr (Sanwa Bank Building), Robert Graham (Ahmanson Headquarters), Beverly Pepper (CalEPA Headquarters), Lita Albuquerque (All Faiths Chapel at Chapman University), Susan Narduli (All Faiths Chapel at Chapman University and Fresno State Library), and Do Ho Suh (Wilshire Grand Center).

Do Ho Suh
Screen, 2017
Wilshire Grand Center
900 Wilshire Boulevard
Los Angeles, CA

BUII
W

TORK

WILSHIRE GRAND CENTER
Los Angeles, California 2017

Rising 1,100 feet above street level, the 75-story Wilshire Grand is the gleaming beacon of the Los Angeles skyline. A mixed-use tower, it features office and retail spaces, restaurants, meeting rooms, a ballroom, and recreational amenities. The 889-room InterContinental Los Angeles Downtown Hotel occupies its highest floors, featuring a dramatic sky lobby and a rooftop bar with breathtaking 360-degree views.

As for the tower's form, David's design inspiration came from Yosemite National Park, with its massive sloping rocks. The industrialized manufacturing world, specifically the aircraft industry, left its mark as well. There's no mistaking the tower's reference to an immense wing.

> As the design evolved, we ended up with geometries on the south elevation and the central skylight that involved parametric curves; that is, curves that wrap and warp in different directions. This marked the first time we had dealt with such geometries, and while the embedded knowledge of the staff at AC Martin was very inventive in computer drawings and techniques, this was a new experience. Every floor plan was different. Every section and every elevation was different. On a 75-story building, the iterations were plentiful.
>
> We had assembled several recent graduates who had each utilized parametric modeling in their college studies. They knew the technology and computational techniques to deal with the subject matter, but had little experience in architectural detailing. The older, experienced architects were experts at detailing, but had never dealt with parametric design before. This brought about an unusual circumstance where the young graduates were leading the charge to evolve the design into the construction drawings.
>
> By the end of the project, we had this marvelous blending of young personnel gaining insight into how to put a building together piece by piece, and the embedded knowledge of the firm being expanded into parametric design in a wonderful way. I believe this is indicative of how things will go in the future. The digital natives will play a major leadership role with new technology, moving into an environment where the exchange between younger and older generations of architects enhances the overall professional experience.

Spatial organization and circulation were key design considerations. Hotel and other public functions are separated efficiently from office lease space via double-decked, high-speed elevators. Vehicular circulation takes advantage of the Wilshire Grand's placement on an entire city block, allowing access from two major streets.

The mechanical system is unique in that each floor has its own circulation system, with intake on the windward side and exhaust on the leeward side. Many of the hotel's guestrooms have operable windows. At ground level, all meeting spaces feature natural light, and the main conference room has access to an adjoining garden.

Artwork is located throughout the Wilshire Grand, most notably *Screen*, a monumental piece by South Korean artist Do Ho Suh. Located in the main lobby, it features 86,000 multi-colored, miniature human figures. The hotel's guestrooms have artistic touches referring to architectural critic Reyner Banham and his "four ecologies" of L.A.: the beach, flatlands, foothills, and freeways; but with the interior design team's addition of a fifth ecology: L.A.'s downtown culture.

Special thanks to our client, Cho Yang-Ho, Chairman and CEO of Korean Air, and his daughter, Heather, who brought their good taste, global ideas, and worldwide experiences with mixed-use developments to the project. At the request of Chairman Cho and his family, AC Martin served as both Development Manager and Architect. Martin Project Management, led by my cousin, Chris Martin, provided the developer services. Tammy Jow, Project Director, led a team of approximately 50 people. Chris King, Interior Design Lead, Carey McLeod, Project Principal, and George vanGilluwe, Project Architect, were all instrumental to the project's tremendous success. — DCM

The tower consists of offices, restaurants, and hotel accommodations. The podium component includes ballrooms, commercial kitchen, mechanical equipment, and pool deck.

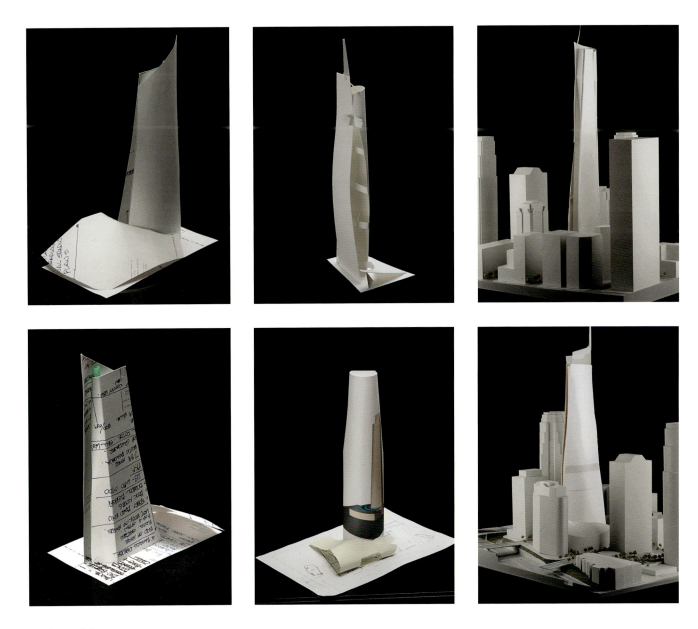

Study Models

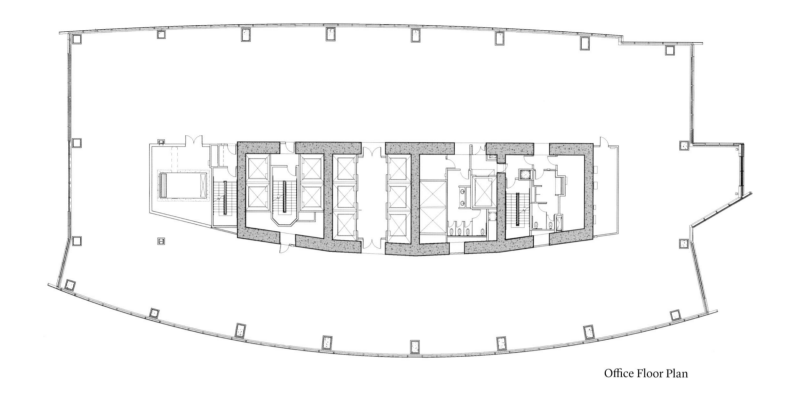

Office Floor Plan

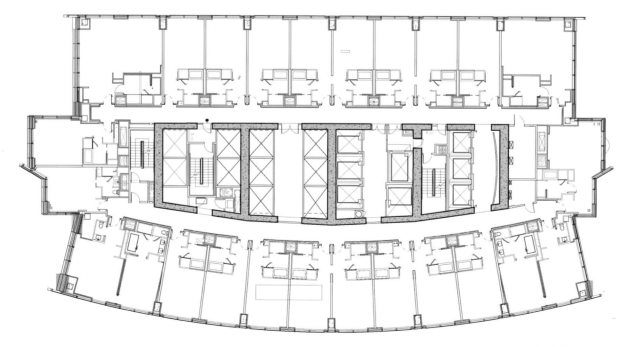

Hotel Floor Plan

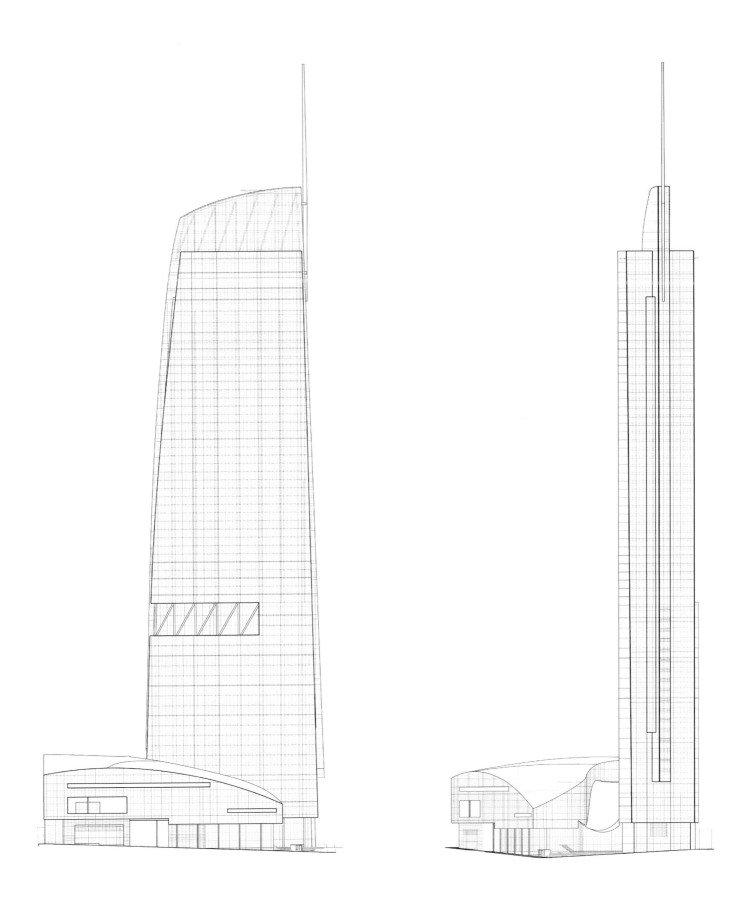

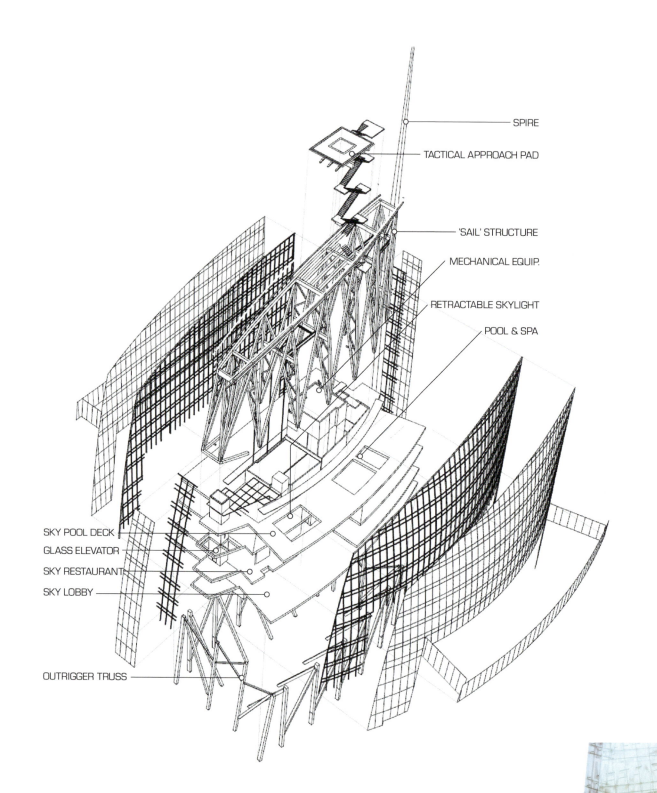

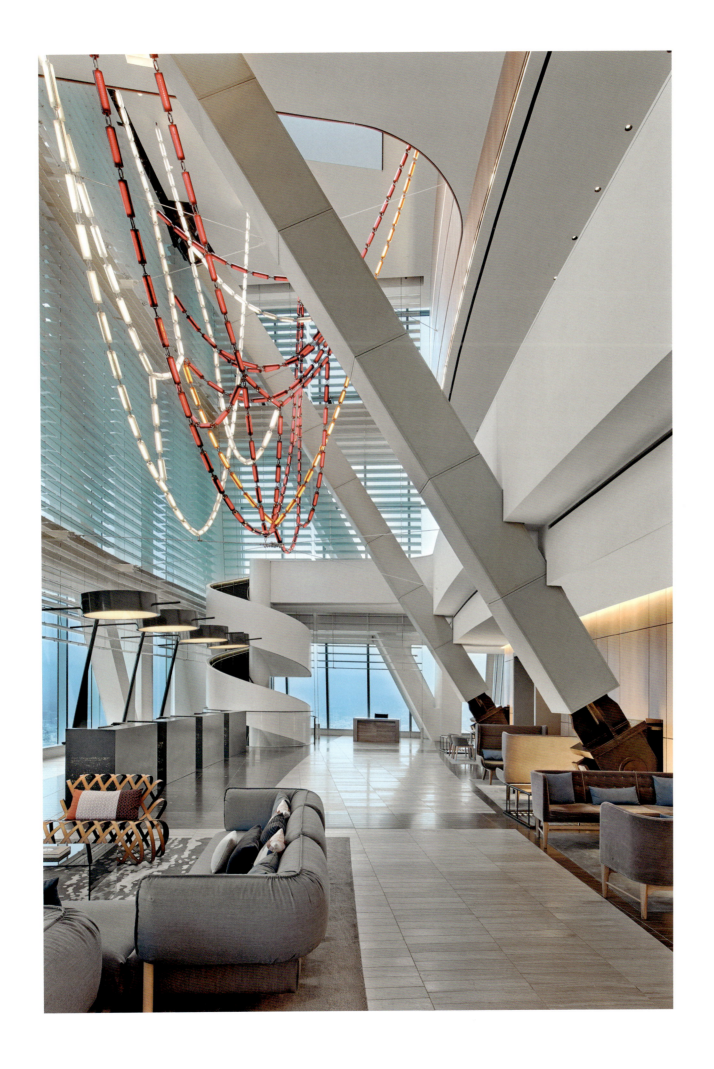

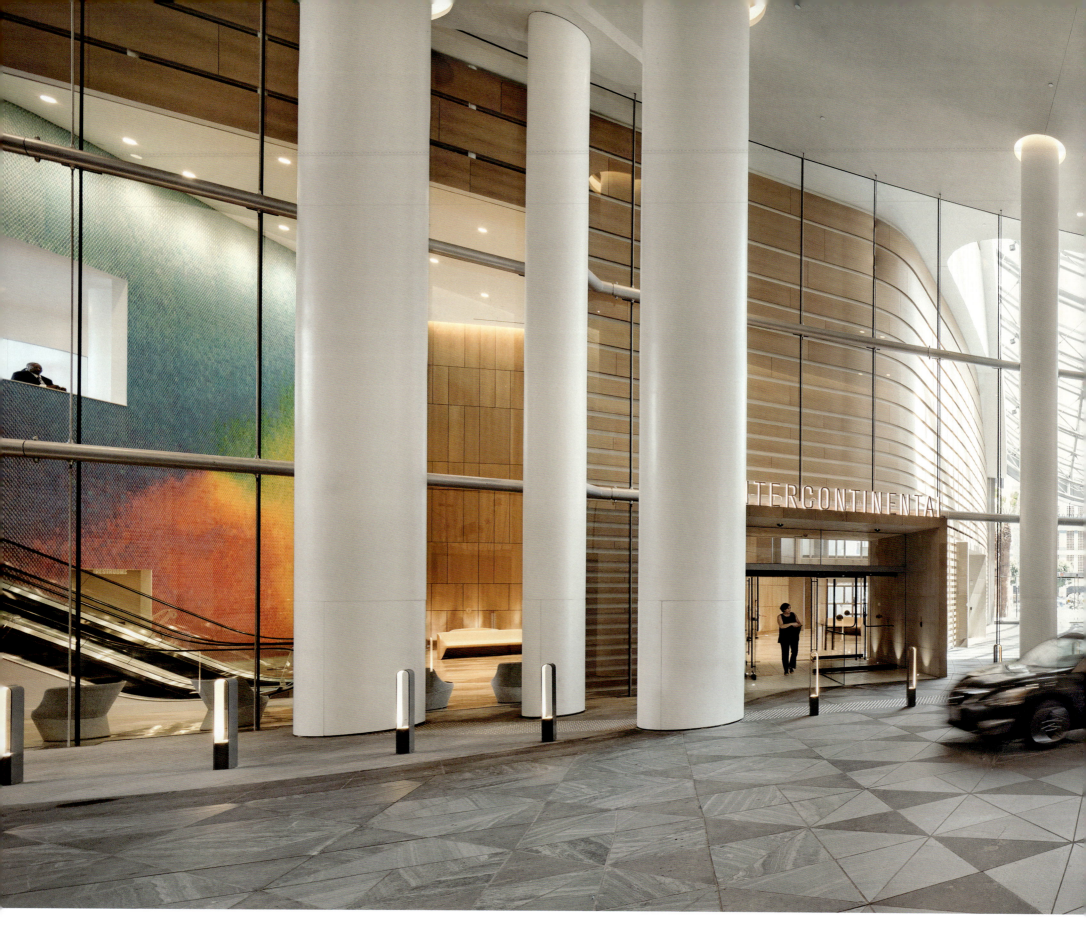
Valet porte cochere for hotel, offices, restaurants, and ballrooms.

The installation, *Screen,* by artist Do Ho Suh, is comprised of 86,000 miniature human figures covering three large walls of the tower's lobby.

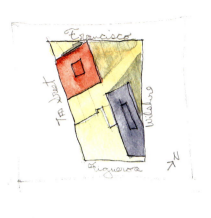

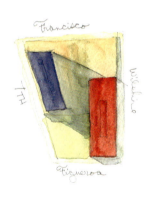

Early sun studies to assure sunlight would reach the plaza at midday throughout the year.

david c. martin
design principal & co-chairman

PROJECT CREDITS

Client
Korean Air

Designers
David C. Martin, Tammy Jow,
Jon Starr, Noel Moreno, Isaac Luna,
Joseph Varholick

**Interior Designers
and Production Staff**
Christopher King, Grit Pasker,
Sandra Lévesque, Michelle Sterling,
Edmund Lau, Naoko Miyano,
Lily Chung, Ryan Petersen,
Inga Newsom, Jessica Houlemard,
Rachel Eisner, Elisa De Dios-Hernandez,
Jorge Medrano, Melanie Gutierrez,
Araceli Gomez, Melisa Sharpe,
Lalida Nakatani, Gerardo Ramirez,
Gary Broeker, Kumiko Matsuda

Project Architects
George vanGilluwe, Tim Redmond,
Peter Kim

Chairman/CEO
Christopher C. Martin

Project Principal
Carey McLeod

Project Director
Tammy Jow

Development Manager
Martin Project Management

Contractor
Turner Construction Company

Structural Engineer
Brandow & Johnston,
Thornton Tomasetti

MEP Engineer
Glumac

SUPERIOR COURT OF CALIFORNIA
COUNTY OF MADERA

Madera, California 2015

Customarily, courthouses are steeped in ancient times, incorporating iconic elements symbolic of their power. The Madera Superior Court embodies instead a unique history connected to the nearby Sierra Nevada mountain range. Its legacy derives from laws relating to mining and timber operations and, ultimately, people visiting the Sierras.

We first met with a committee of the Court's judges to register their thoughts and set a direction for the design. Right off the bat, one of the judges stood up and said, in essence, 'We're not interested in the classic Greco-Roman interpretation of a courthouse, with its grand steps, colonnade, portico, and pediment. That wouldn't mean anything to this community.'

This judge had the vision that the building should be composed of stone and granite to represent the majestic cliffs and stone faces of the valley, that glass should be incorporated to symbolize the area's waterfalls and ice formations, and that there should be lots of timber inside to represent its tremendous importance to the history of Madera, the San Joaquin Valley, and California. And that was it. It was so moving to hear this poetic description of how one might go about carrying on the history of this courthouse. And, of course, it was a fabulous idea, so we proceeded along those lines.

David and the design team focused on producing a public experience grounded in warmth, safety, views, and daylight, utilizing local, natural materials. The team paid special attention to making a visual connection between the new courthouse and the original courthouse located across the street. The building features four courtroom modules, with a glass-lined atrium at its core. This transparent element reveals an interior predicated on warmth, with a wood-clad lobby and beautifully-detailed treatments gracing the space.

We chose to clad the courtroom modules with Sierra White granite from the Raymond Quarry, just 12 miles from the project site. It's a historic granite that was used in a lot of the early public buildings in California.

One of the problems with Sierra White is that it's so absolutely consistent, and the grain is rather fine. When you cut it into panels, from a distance, it almost looks like plywood or cardboard. It doesn't retain much of its stone character if not carved or applied to the orders of architecture.

Working with my colleague Tammy Jow, we knew about this, and we started to explore what would happen if you slightly tilted each panel. Tammy developed a system for achieving this without adding tremendous complexity to the detailing process, working closely with the quarry staff and our curtain wall experts.

Tammy and I both happen to be musicians, so we realized we could also make a pattern with the panels. In conversations, we said, 'Gee, we could make music! We could deliver a message by basically having the panels move in and out at different degrees, becoming a system of numbers ordered to match the tab patterns of a musical note sequence.' We decided that it would be great to have this hidden jazz pattern traversing the entire courthouse. The result was a series of chord fingerlings: Am7 - D7 - Gma7 - Cma7 - F#m7bt - B7 Em7 - E7. It is a classic II V I jazz chord progression. I don't think anybody would ever pick that out, but that's how it happened.

The building is designed to accommodate future expansion, thanks to its modular components. It currently includes ten courtrooms and ten judicial chambers, along with spaces for jury services, prisoner holding, vehicle accommodations, and support areas.

The design process was a wonderful example of collaboration among the Judicial Council of California, the Madera County Superior Court administration, three judges led by the Hon. Charles A. Wieland, and Bonnie Thomas, Court Executive Officer. All were hands-on participants. Tammy Jow maintained the design contract, kept the client happy, and met the required cost parameters. — DCM

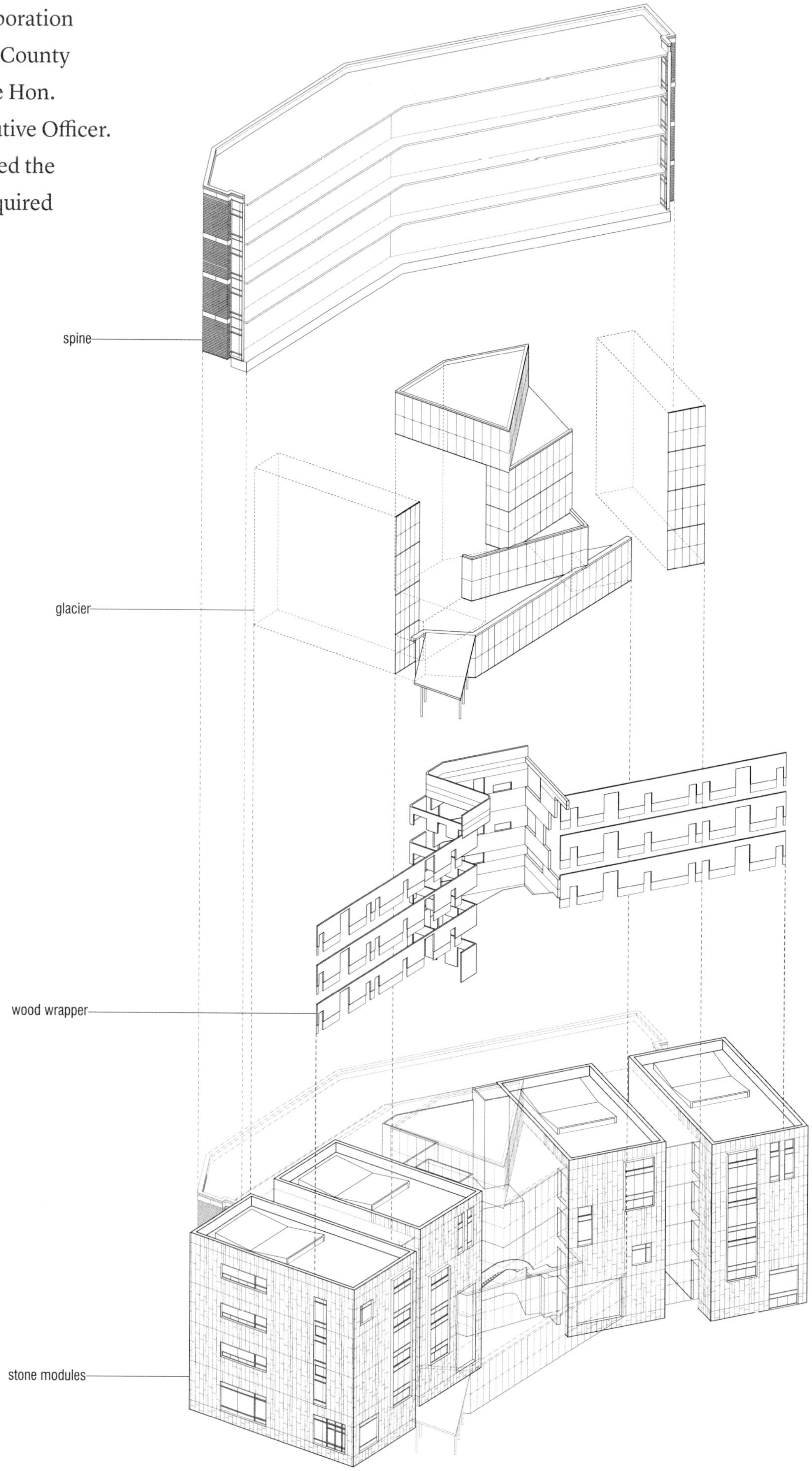

spine

glacier

wood wrapper

stone modules

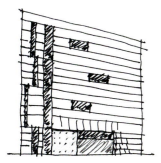 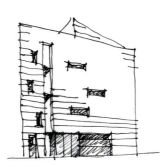 

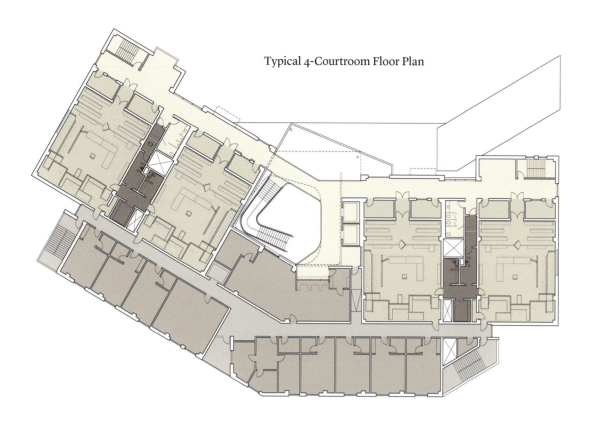

Typical 4-Courtroom Floor Plan

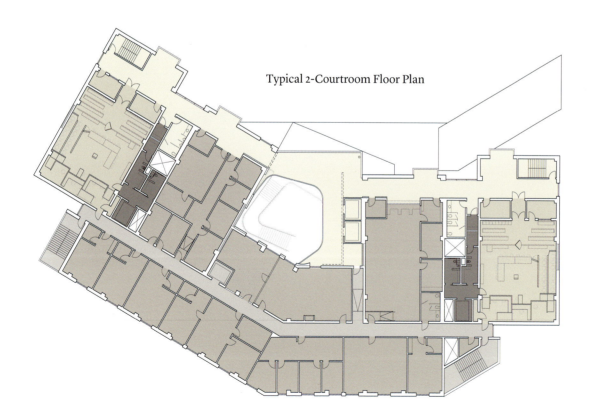

Typical 2-Courtroom Floor Plan

Light Tan - Public Areas
Medium Tan - Courtrooms
Dark Tan - Chambers and Related
Support Facilities

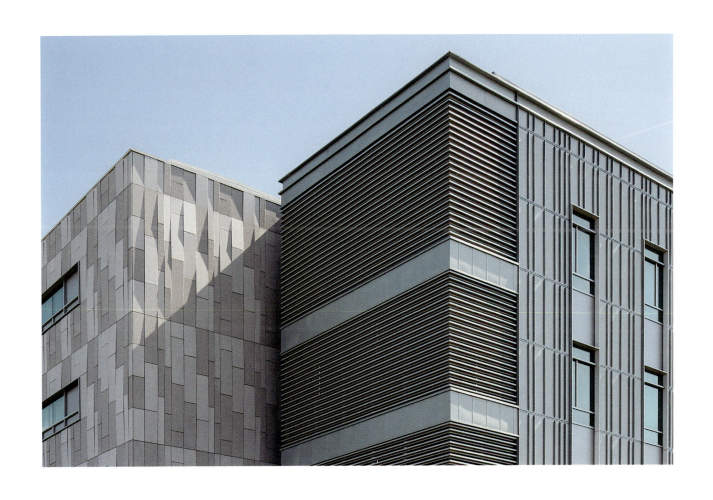

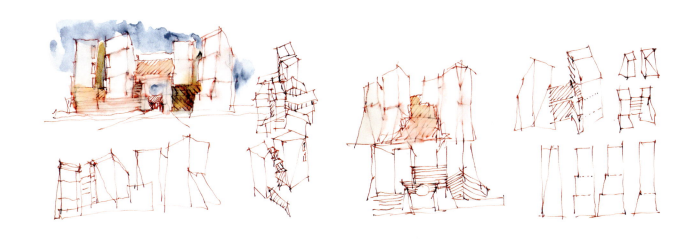

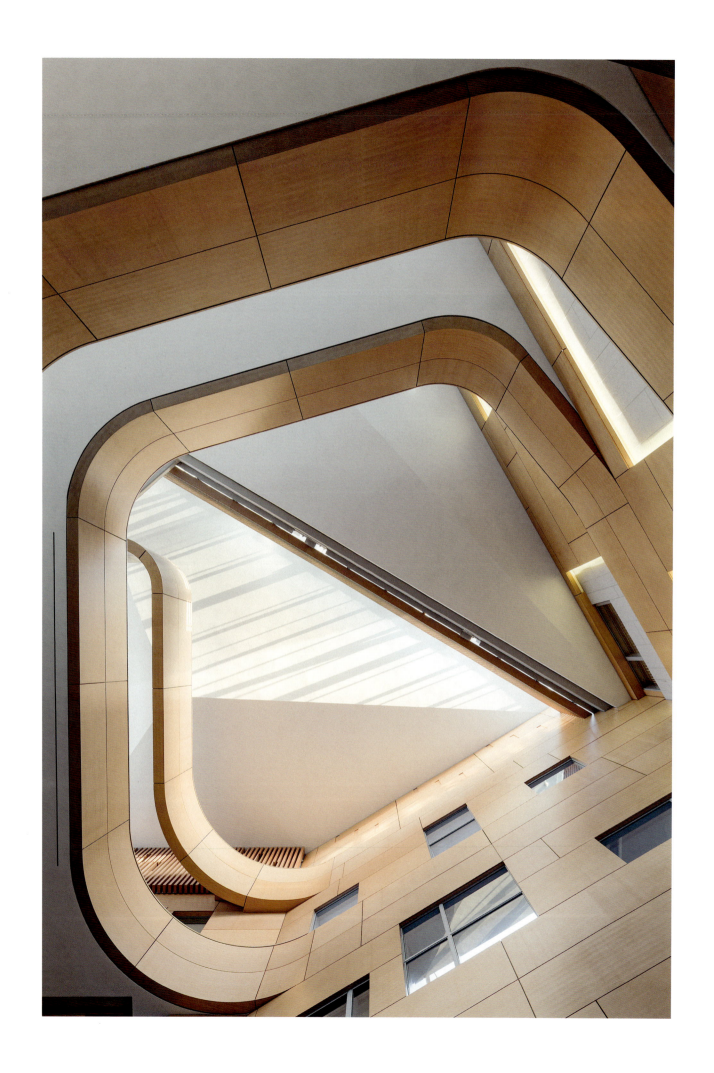

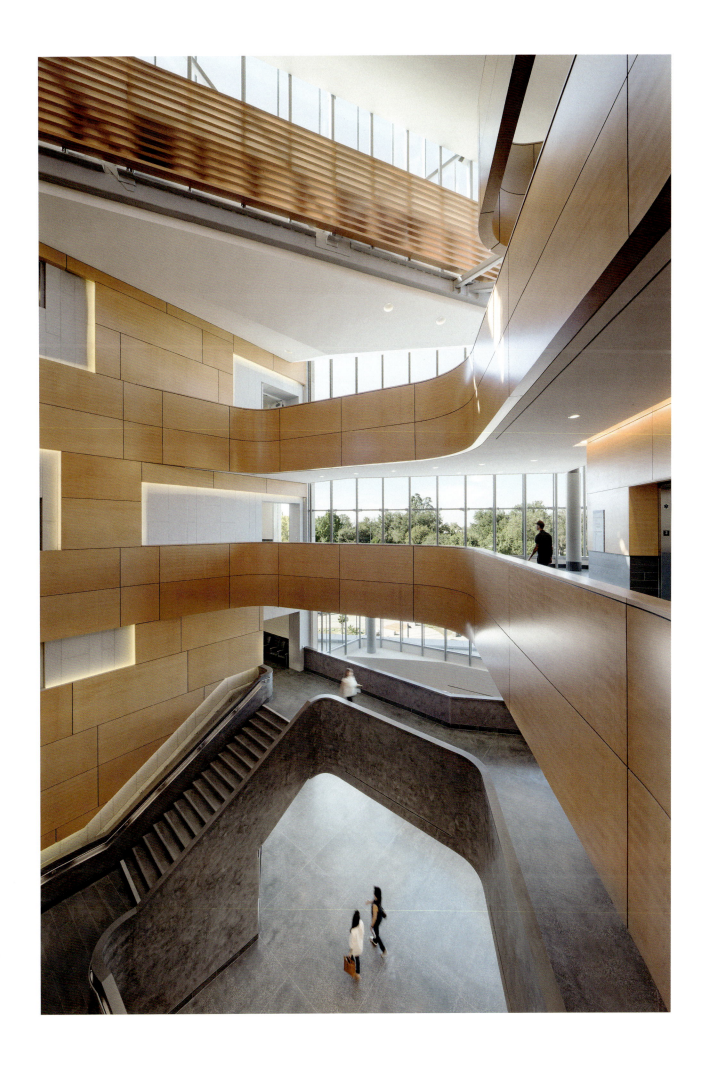

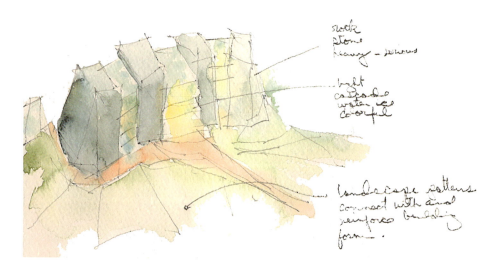

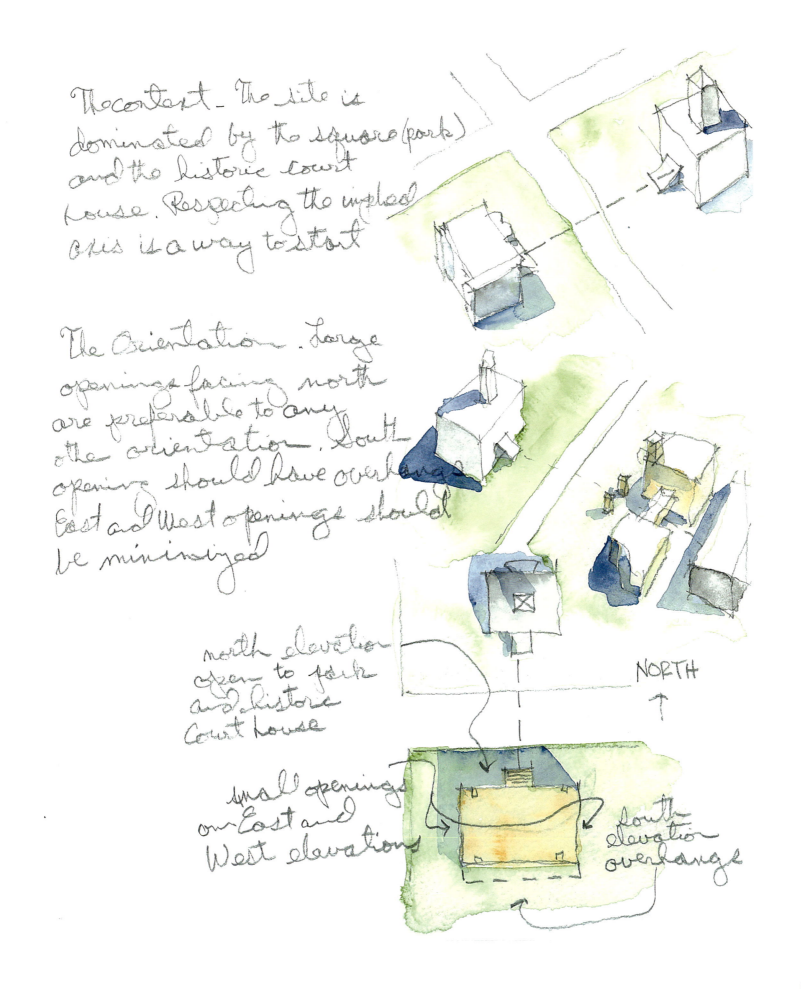

The context - The site is dominated by the square (park) and the historic court house. Respecting the implied axis is a way to start.

The Orientation. Large openings facing north are preferable to any other orientation. South openings should have overhangs. East and West openings should be minimized.

north elevation open to park and historic court house

small openings on East and West elevations

south elevation overhang

NORTH ↑

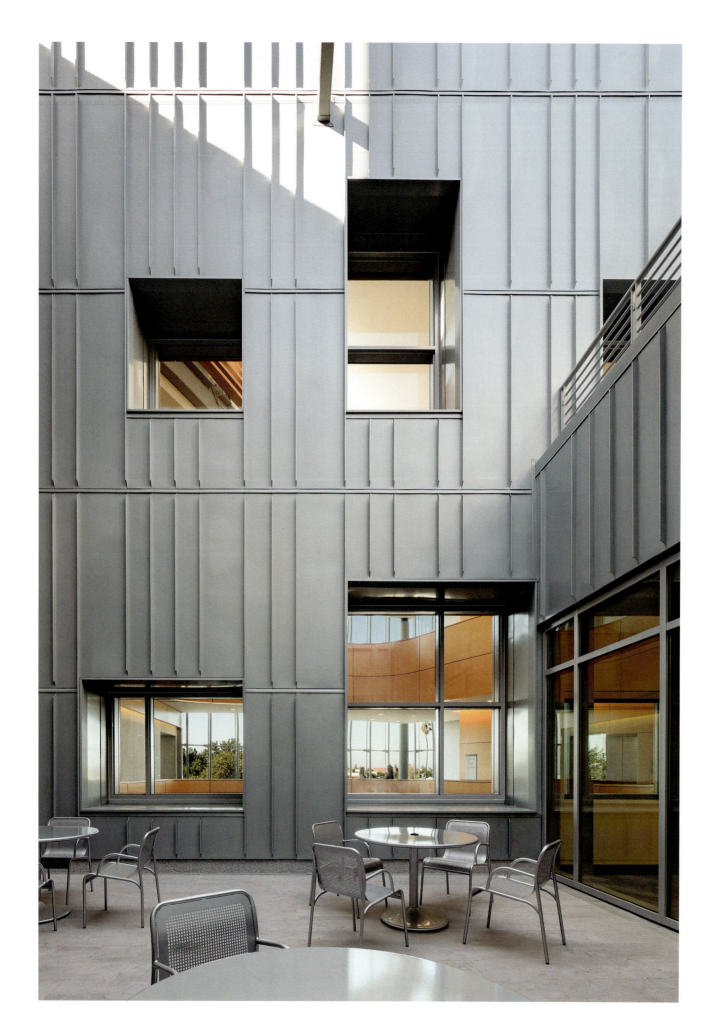
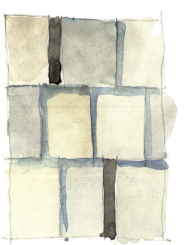

GRANITE SHINGLES WITH
SMALL STAIR WINDOWS

4 COURT CLUSTERS   RAYMOND GRANITE

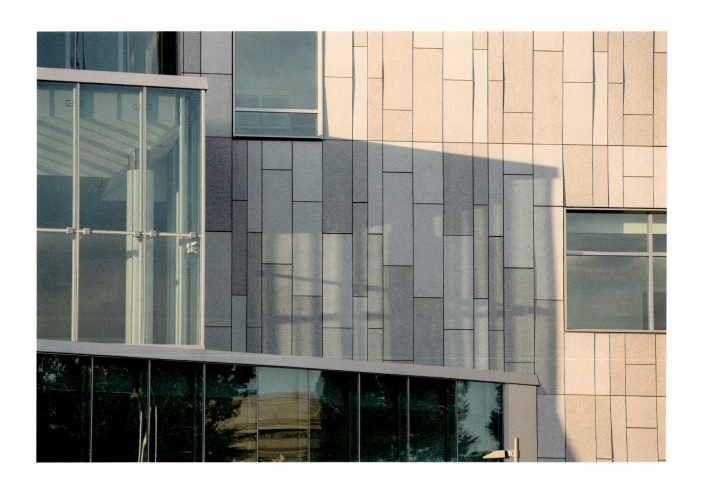

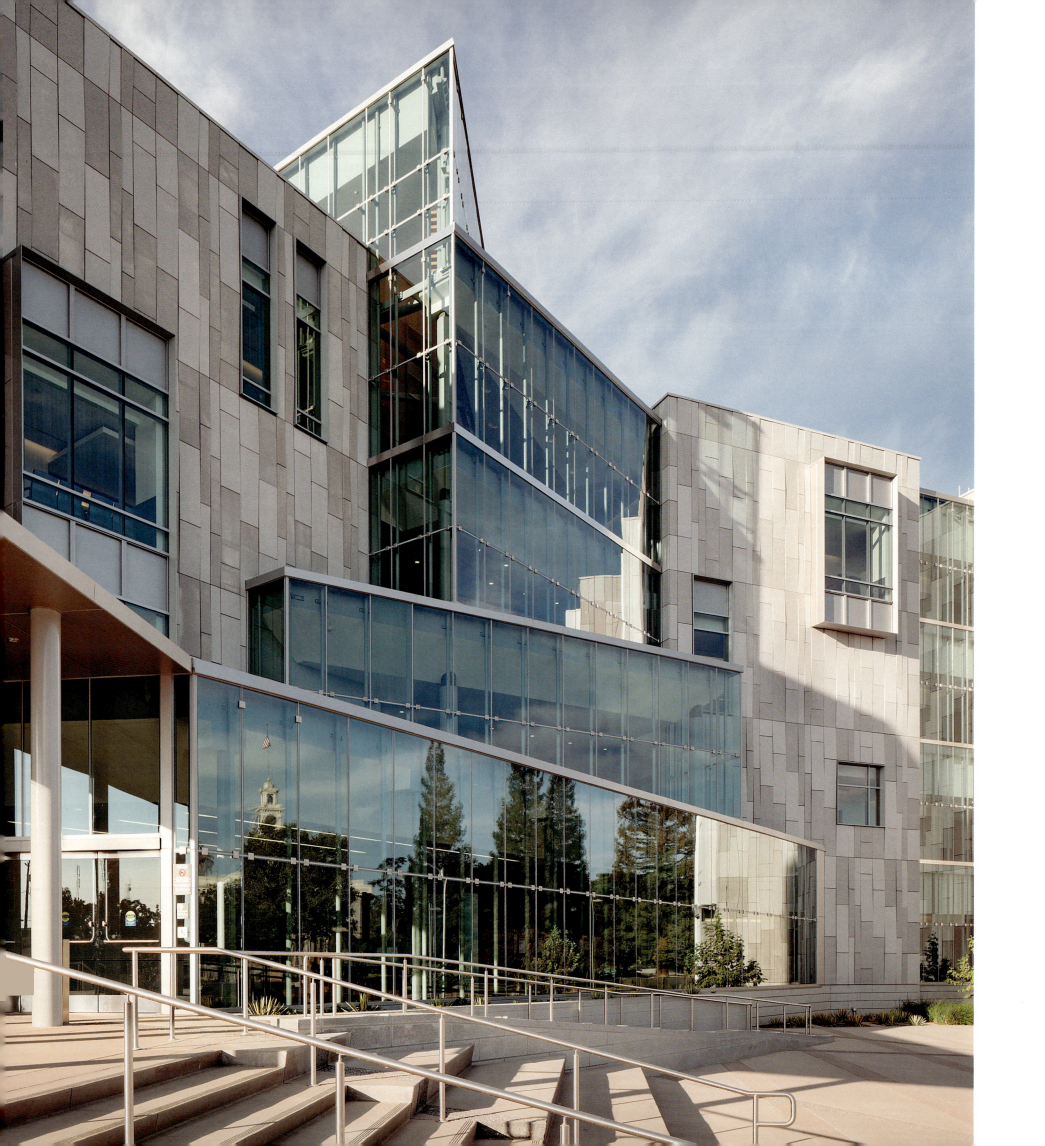

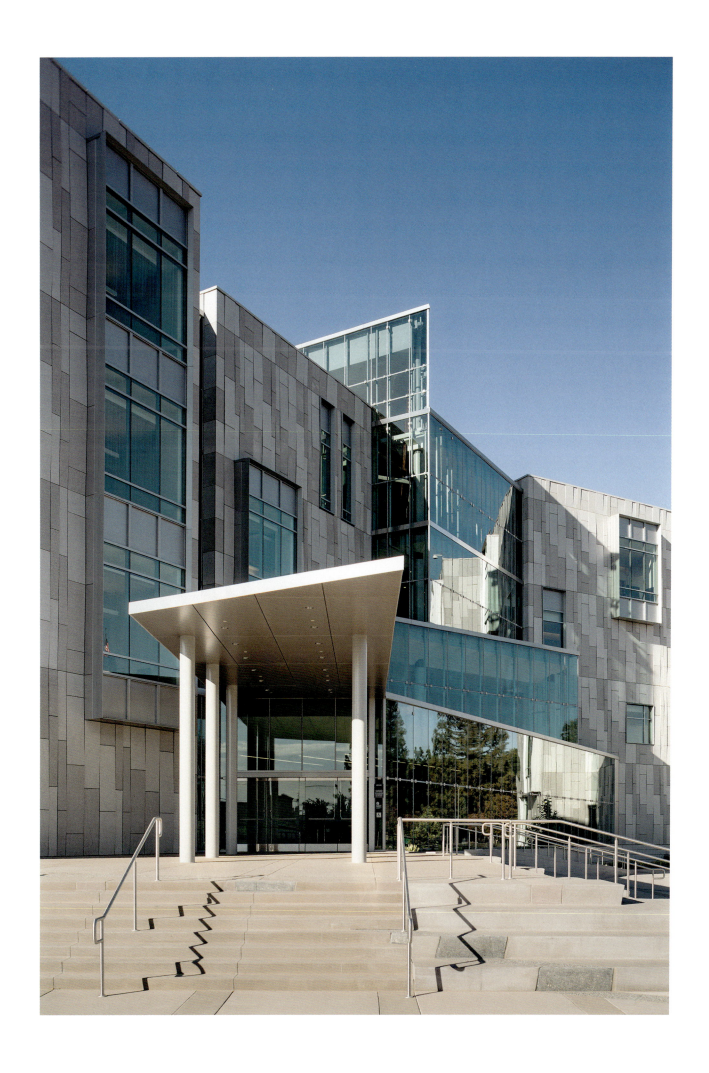

PROJECT CREDITS

Client
Judicial Council of California

Designers
David C. Martin, Tammy Jow

Interior Designers
Sandra Lévesque, Grit Pasker

Project Architects
Tim Redmond, Peter Kim

Project Manager
Doug Fisher

Project Principal
Carey McLeod

Contractor
Tammy Jow

Development Manager
Martin Project Management

Contractor
Gilbane Building Company

Structural Engineer
Brandow & Johnston / AC Martin

MEP Engineer
Glumac

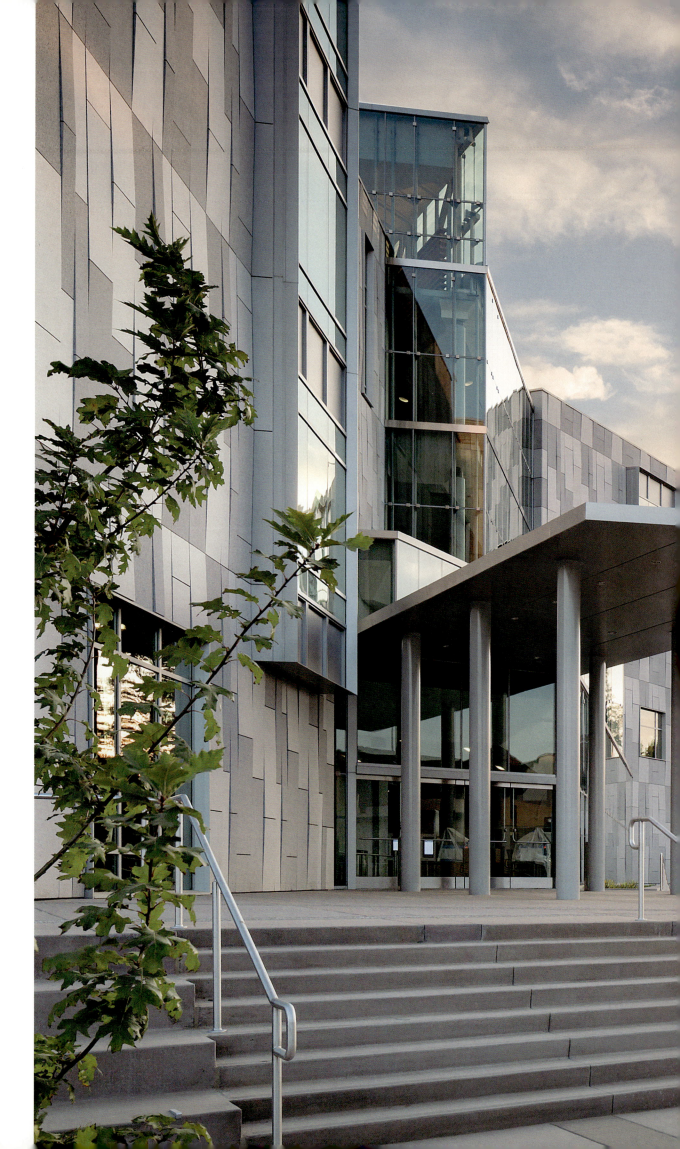

CALIFORNIA STATE UNIVERSITY, FRESNO
FRESNO STATE LIBRARY
Fresno, California 2009

The library at California State University, Fresno, goes beyond being a repository for books and a learning experience for students, faculty, and the community. It is a campus landmark, symbolically linked to this Central California town and its rich history.

Among the library's patrons is the Table Mountain Rancheria, a local Native American tribe whose land lies at the foot of the Sierras. As part of the design process, David visited with tribal elders to learn about their methods of living, both in pre-historic times and the present day. This experience revealed the tribe's expertise in basket weaving, which David used as inspiration for the library's entry piece.

> To mark the front door of the library, I inserted a 5-story high, elliptical form composed of diagonal wood sheathing. In design progress meetings, I was often asked why I would do that and the meaning of it. I was never able to explain myself very well. But one day, they asked me again. I blurted out that it symbolized a basket woven by one of the nearby native tribes —a basket containing knowledge. And that's all it took. They said, 'Oh!' and never asked again.

To expand upon the tribal significance, David and artist Susan Narduli devoted a portion of the building's exterior wall to a 43-foot-tall digital media screen. It presents a film of master basket weaver Lois Conner assembling a gambling basket. Documenting Conner's process in real-time, the film covers a full academic year, so students can watch the "lady in red" and determine the time of year according to the progression of the basket's completion.

Another significant feature of the building is its long, glazed façade along the north elevation. This transparent wall allows light to penetrate deep into the library's stacks and storage areas, as well as provide beautiful views of the adjacent Peace Garden. The precast concrete structure is patterned to reflect the area's surrounding fields and how the land is tilled.

Inside, the library has mostly open-plan floors, offering study and seating choices, including lounge-like options and built-in seating on the grand staircase. Technology is embedded into the scheme, enhancing the library's functions with a view to the future. Innovations include embedded microchips for book tracking and compact movable stacks to allow for additional volumes over time.

Working with the elders of the Table Mountain Rancheria was the thrill of my lifetime. Michael Gorman, Dean of Library Services at Fresno State, was a great resource in helping us design library spaces that function best for students of a commuter college. Chris King provided architectural design and interior design collaboration, and the RMJM team provided expert planning and interiors services. — DCM

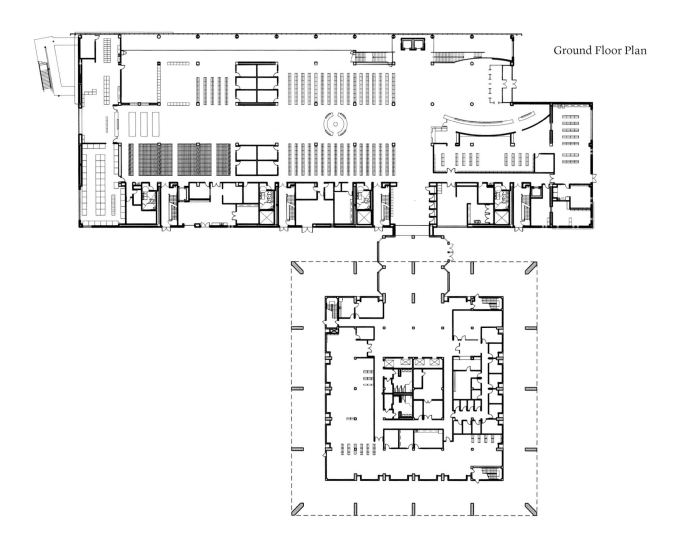

Ground Floor Plan

2nd Level Floor Plan

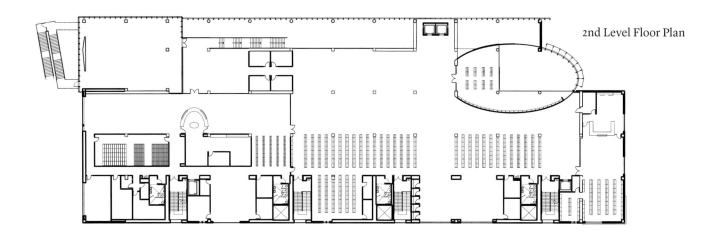

The design solution involved the expansion of the facility to the north.

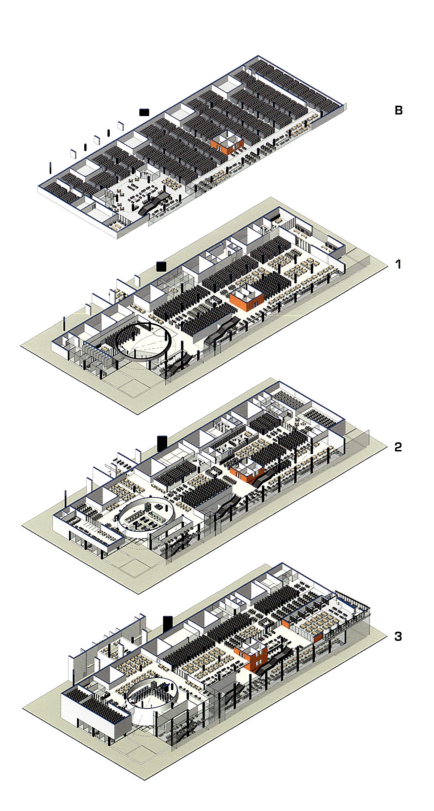
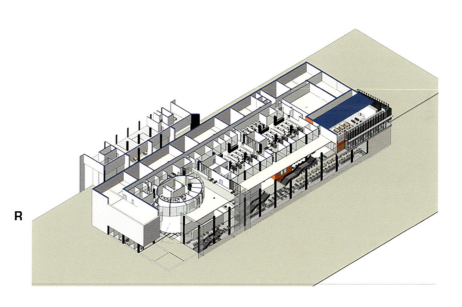

PROJECT CREDITS

Client
California State University, Fresno

Architect of Record/
Structural Engineer
AC Martin

Associate Architect
RMJM Hillier

Designers
David C. Martin, Christopher King

Project Architects
Wat Charoenrath, Peter Kim

Project Principal
Robert R. Murrin

Project Director
Doug Fisher

Contractor
Swinerton Builders

MEP Engineer
Glumac

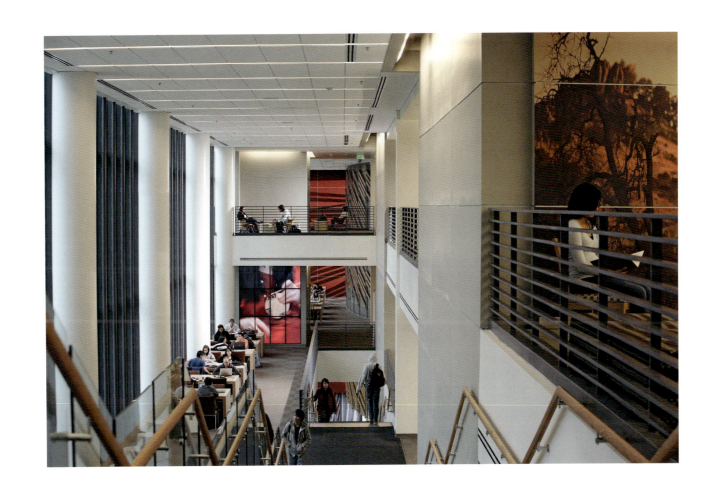

THE FISH INTERFAITH CENTER AT CHAPMAN UNIVERSITY

Orange, California 2004

One of Chapman University's central commitments is openness to diverse religious, spiritual, political, and ethical traditions. In step with this commitment, The Fish Interfaith Center, including The Wallace All Faiths Chapel, sends a message of spirituality versus religiosity. The Center encourages interfaith dialogue and stresses the interconnectedness of humankind.

When we started our discussions with Chapman's chaplain and president, the program was quite clear: This had to be a very welcoming chapel to people of all faiths.

Our first reaction—because this would involve the major religions and then some—was that we would, in some kind of wonderful way, treat the symbols of all these religions much like you would all the flags at a United Nations facility. But we quickly realized that approach would become fraught with problems, symbolizing conflicts and so on, and we quickly moved off of it.

We then asked ourselves: 'What are the elements that bind all of these religions? What do they have in common in terms of ritual, festivities, and doctrine?' And the answer was pretty easy. They all share a special appreciation for the earth, the sun and the stars, nature and water and air and light. The dramatic treatment of each one of these fundamental elements became important to us.

Layered on top of that was the idea that we were creating a spiritual place, a place of worship, and it had to be dramatically different than other spaces on campus. One should move, both literally and figuratively, through a procession that would lead you from that outside world and slowly prepare you for arrival at the spiritual space.

So this "journey to the spiritual" started to take on thoughts of tower as entrance, a pergola going past a marvelous special garden, through a front door, down a colonnaded space that at first had clear windows to the outdoors, followed by windows that started to become more translucent than transparent, and moving through a series of lower passages into the spiritual space, which would ultimately reveal itself to be that place of light and air and water.

And with that thinking came the notion that we would involve many artists who would help us celebrate that journey. They would create elemental features of each one of those processional spaces and help us prepare one to leave a rather material world with all of its jazz and goings-on and enter a very special and different kind of place. These artists (Susan Narduli, Lita Albuquerque, Nori Sato, Richard Turner, and William Tunberg) designed sacred gardens in the walkways and passageways, sculptural and poetic forms, and actual poetry embedded in the walkways and at the end of vistas. They addressed materiality of the door handles and passages at the door, and once inside the large place of worship, pendants representing stars, sculptures representing clouds, windows with special characteristics that would emphasize the qualities of light entering into the space, and chairs with stunning marquetry alluding to the galaxies.

When we returned years later, we witnessed how successful the Center truly is. There is an absolute acceptance of a Catholic mass, followed by a Jewish ritual, for example. All faiths are welcome and celebrated. I think, most importantly, it has become a place of rest and reflection for the students who drop by throughout the day to get themselves into another kind of mental framework.

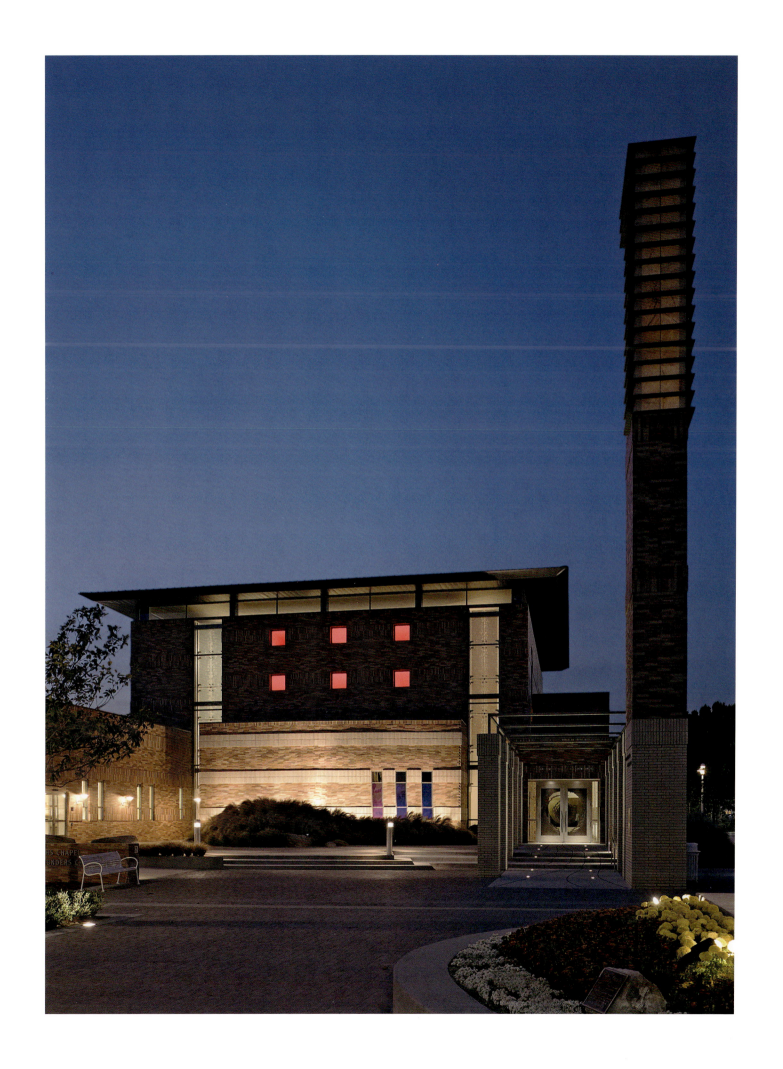

I thank James Doti, President of Chapman University, for his guidance in adhering to the design standards established by the Old Town Historical Guidelines of the City of Orange. Thanks also go to Kris Olsen, Vice President, Campus Planning and Operations at Chapman University, and Theresia Kurnadi, who worked closely with me throughout the design process. — DCM

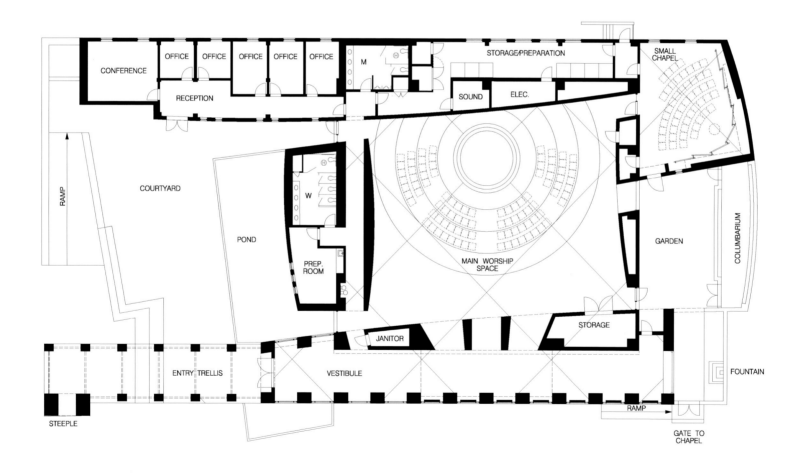

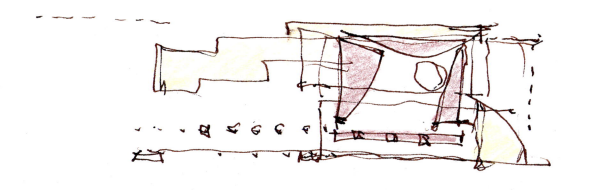

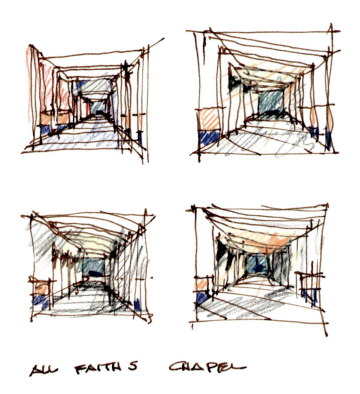

ALL FAITHS CHAPEL

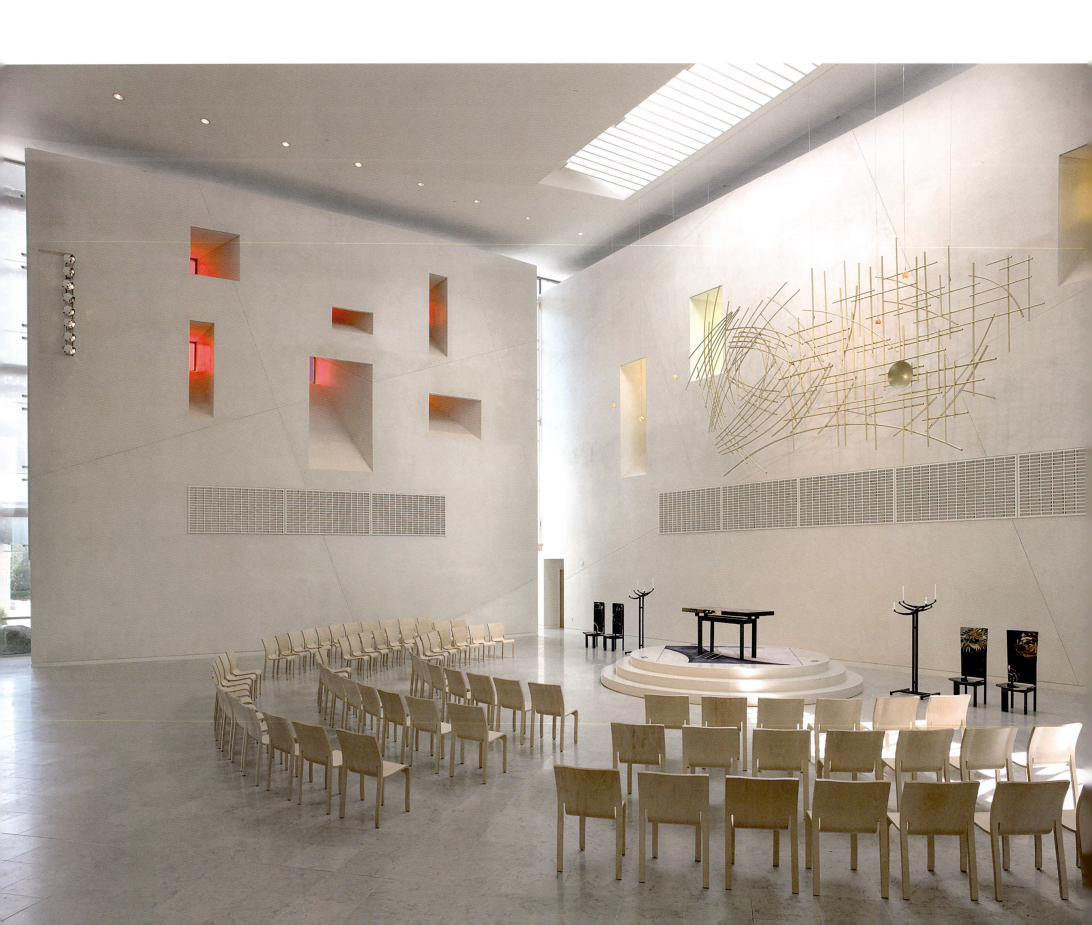

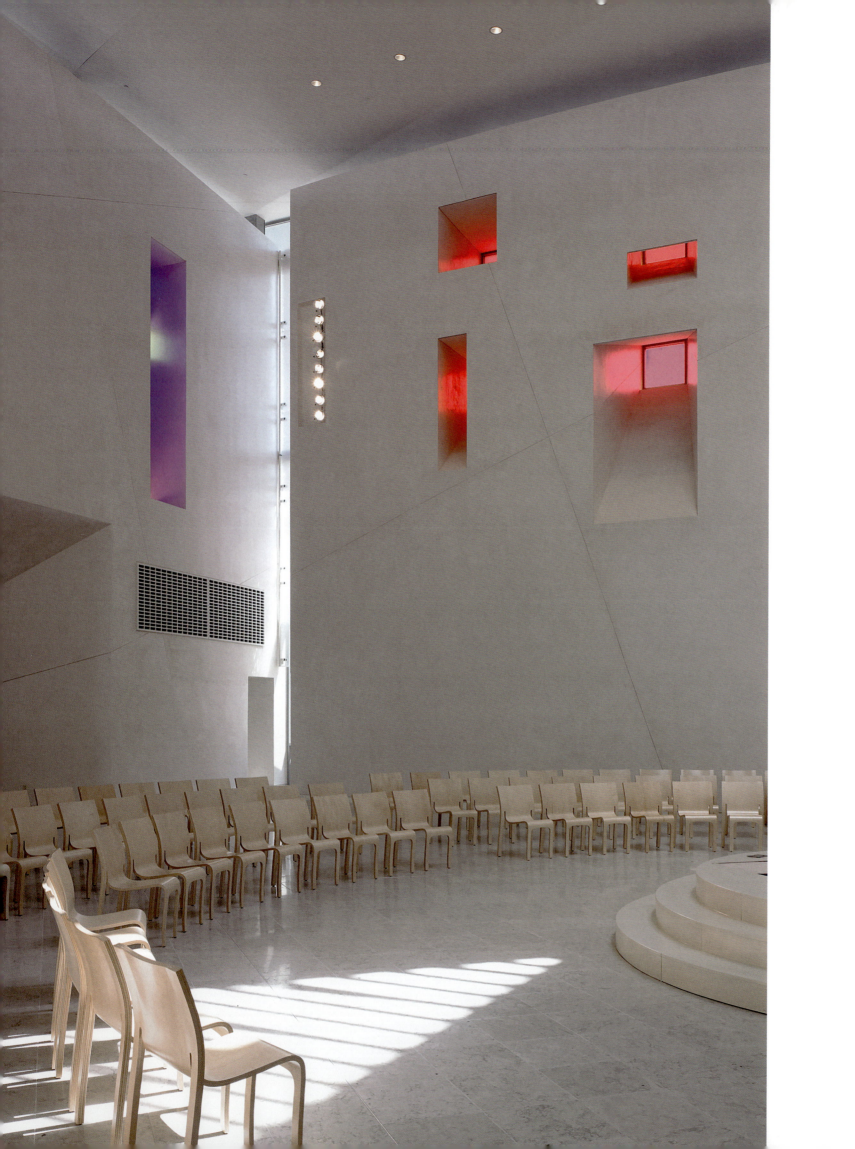

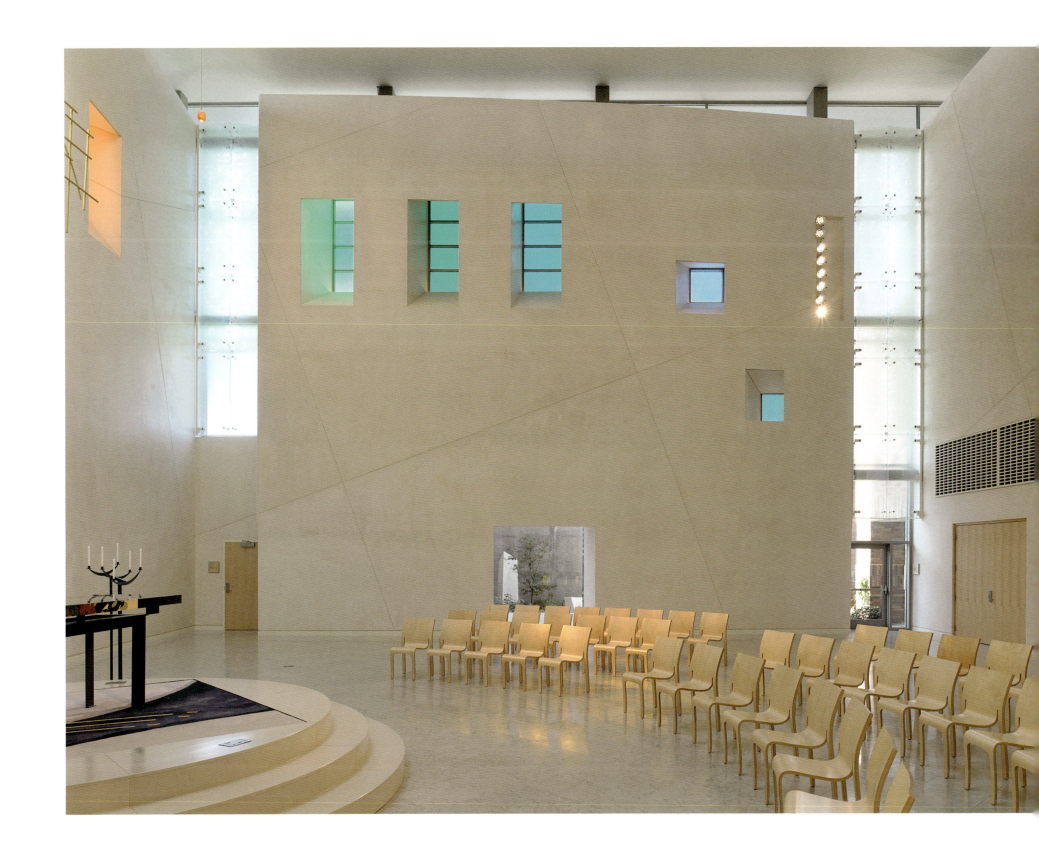

Furnishing details

David collaborated with artist William Tunberg in the design of these altar chairs. The striking marquetry patterns were inspired by images from the Hubbell Space Telescope. Each chair's ornament is unique.

PROJECT CREDITS

Client
Chapman University

Designers
David C. Martin, Theresia Kurnadi

Project Architect
Norm Title

Project Principal
Robert R. Murrin

Contractor
Snyder Langston

Structural Engineer
AC Martin

MEP Engineer
M-E Engineers

The Garden of the Senses (right) and columbarium (opposite) were designed by artist Susan Narduli. The columbarium is sculpted of Brazilian marble.

HOLLENBECK COMMUNITY POLICE STATION

Boyle Heights, California 2009

The City of Los Angeles passed a bond to redesign 13 of its aging police stations.

> We competed very hard for this job. We were among really good architects, and the process was really tough. We did very well in the interviews and came out at the top of the City's list of selected architects. For this reason, we were offered the first choice of station. While there were some in upscale neighborhoods where quality and materials would be important, we opted instead for the station in Boyle Heights. It has gentrified quite a bit since then, but at the time, it was a rough and tough part of the world. It was notorious for shootings, murder, drugs, and the like. And that was its appeal. It provided us with a great design challenge.

The design team was excited to have the opportunity to make a meaningful contribution to the Boyle Heights community. The unexpected thrill was the artistic freedom the representatives of the Hollenbeck Division and their wonderful Captain, Anita Ortega, granted the team.

> One of the big issues, and a politically-charged one at the time, was the transparency of the LAPD. The Department's effectiveness at interacting with the communities they served was being closely examined. As we were developing programmatic material, we got to work closely with Hollenbeck representatives. We went on ride-alongs in police cruisers. We began to understand the good and bad characteristics of the neighborhood. We also attended a graduation ceremony at the Police Academy. It was really a thrill for me to see these dedicated people being recognized amid the splendor of a positive, military-style graduation.

The police station was located across the street from a park—not necessarily a pleasant one—it was a drug park that happened to be operating in the shadow of the station. But it proved the point that transparency was an agenda that had to be pushed. Our design scheme literally made the interface begin at the front desk, where the community meets with police officers and other representatives. We made that an all-glass statement, and not just basic glass panes, but rather a sculptured, translucent, inviting glass building facade that spoke directly to transparency and hope, and accessibility. Good things could indeed happen here.

The Hollenbeck representatives were thrilled that the design team would provide a solution so tailored to their specific station, a solution that met their staff's daily needs but was also artistic and engaging. This was certainly not typical, since the general tendency was to make police stations look like fortresses, to provide a sense of security and strength and protection, but also suggesting a confrontational barrier between the police and their surrounding community. That said, there were certainly concerns raised about security.

> While the design concept sounded appealing to the majority, the question was posed: "How do we protect the officer at the head desk?" People had been known to shoot at the police station. That was part of the history of this place. So we went to great lengths to understand how this facility had to be bulletproof. You couldn't be able to recognize anybody if you were driving by. We overcame these issues with the help of security analysts and by utilizing special materials throughout the building. We tested the material compositions at a shooting range to be sure that they really did work.

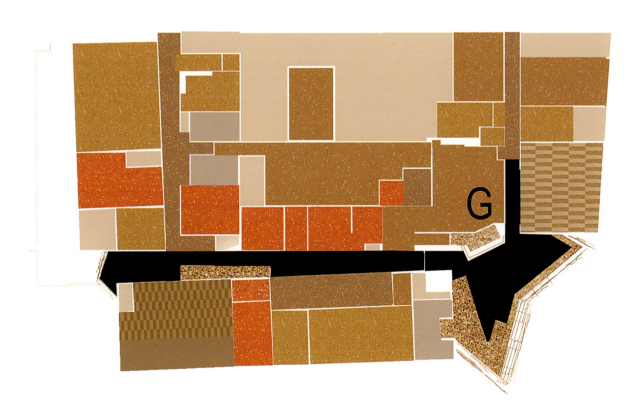

Programming diagrams depicting ground floor public receiving area and community rooms, and 2nd floor detectives' offices, gymnasium, and locker rooms.

The building serves as a safe haven, with access to ATMs and meeting spaces for events. A vibrant mural is included in the design, alluding to the neighborhood's tradition of brightly-colored houses, gardens, and murals. All help to stitch the station into the community fabric.

> These kinds of places lead to success. It was well-received by the neighborhood. Some thought it should be in the Spanish style or reflect back on other times, but there was another part of the community that just said, 'No. This is not Santa Barbara. This is someplace unique, and we should pick up on that vibe and that excitement that does exist in this neighborhood.' And since then, in terms of crime, the positive aspects of the neighborhood and its streets have continued to improve.

Thank you to the City of Los Angeles for its bond program that engendered a professional and creative process benefiting many neighborhoods. Credit also goes to the personnel of the Hollenbeck station. They were intently interested and active participants in the design process, resulting in something truly special for themselves and their neighborhood. Thanks also go to Tammy Jow, who was responsible for the space plan and the organization and implementation of the design; Chris King, who was particularly helpful in the design of the glass fenestration and entryway; and Carey McLeod, Project Manager. — DCM

PROJECT CREDITS

Client
City of Los Angeles

Designers
David C. Martin. Christopher King,
Tammy Jow

Interior Designer
Elizabeth Eshel

Project Architect
Norm Title

Project Manager
Carey McLeod

Project Director
Rana Makarem

Construction Manager/Contractor
FTR International

Structural Engineer
AC Martin

MEP Engineer
TMAD

FIFTH DISTRICT COURT OF APPEAL

Fresno, California 2007

Located in Fresno's "Old Armenian Town" district, the Fifth District Court of Appeal is a dignified and meaningful place of justice. It includes a single courtroom plus chambers for ten justices, offices for attorneys and staff, clerk-administrative offices, a library, conference spaces that support appellate courthouse operations, and secured parking.

Appellate courts typically include just one courtroom in the building, with court activity occurring periodically. Strict security measures are upheld, and generally, the courtroom cannot be open to the environment. Windows are discouraged due to the dangers posed by visibility.

> One of the most interesting ideas about the Court of Appeal is that the courtroom, where all of the action and the purpose of the building emanates from, is located in the middle of the building's courtyard on the ground floor. The walls facing the courtyard are filled with glass to bring in natural light and establish a pleasant environment for the intense and intellectual work of the Court. Due to security concerns, very few appellate courts have this kind of connection to the outside world, but it works due to the large interior windows of the atrium space surrounding the courtroom.
>
> I think we broke some ground here in how we set this one up.

The courtyard plan adds to the collegiality of staff within the building, as all can see one another. Each office space receives natural daylight and optimal views.

The limestone-clad building forms an edge to a pedestrian plaza complete with stone bands simulating rows of vines, a wisteria-draped pergola, and a promenade lined with flowering fruit trees. All reference the agrarian tradition of Fresno. When approaching the building, visitors are welcomed by a reflecting pool and immediately see the warm, wood-paneled walls of the public lobby within.

Security measures, both active and passive, pervade the entire site, including parking areas, the perimeter, the entrance, and interior spaces. The facility also features up-to-date data-telecom and audio-visual systems to support infrastructure requirements.

> I thank Administrative Presiding Justice James A. Ardaiz for smoothing the way for our design team. He met with us regularly and provided us with an uninterrupted line of communication with the Court. He was also key to gathering and disseminating information to all stakeholders. And I thank Tammy Jow for another marvelous working experience. — DCM

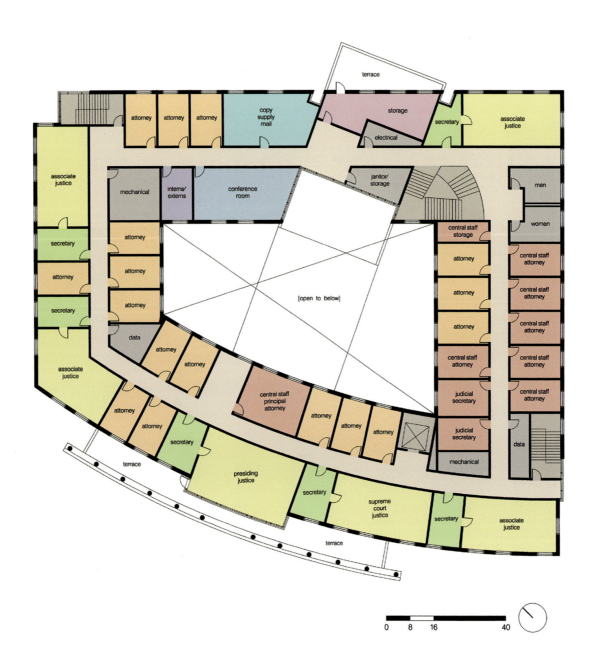

PROJECT CREDITS

Client
Judicial Council of California

Designers
David C. Martin, Tammy Jow

Project Architects
Wat Charoenrath, Prem Encarnacion

Project Director
Carey McLeod

Contractor
Harris Construction

Structural Engineer
AC Martin

MEP Engineer
TRC EASI

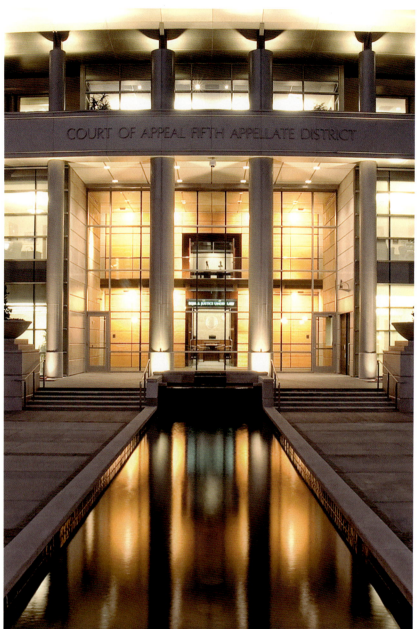

The building's configuration and internal glazing offers the sole courtroom and surrounding administrative offices views of the courtyard garden and an abundance of daylight that benefits both courthouse employees and visitors.

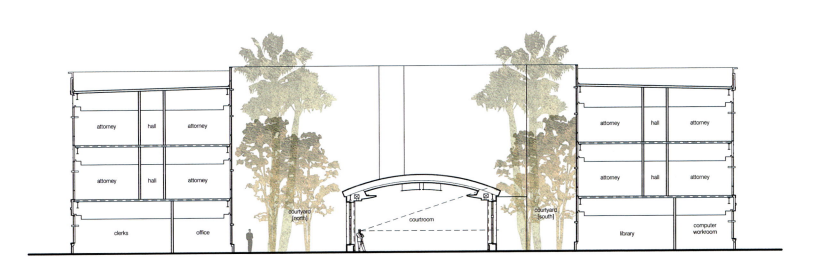

107

UNIVERSITY OF CALIFORNIA, IRVINE HUMANITIES, MUSIC, AND FINE ARTS BUILDINGS
Irvine, California 1999

This complex of three buildings at the University of California, Irvine, brings context to a campus planned by architect William Pereira in the 1960s. The master plan was conceived as a large ring. Academic buildings are arrayed around this ring.

David focused on reinforcing Pereira's historic ring plan to bolster campus connections. He introduced a pedestrian circulation axis to connect the new buildings (located on opposite sides of a roadway) to the ring. The success of the project in terms of the master plan led to other UCI projects following similar strategies.

> We were able to plan, design, and build the three buildings all at the same time. They were located in the same district on campus but not adjacent to one another, and were located along a campus walkway leading from the ring mall out to various peripheral parking structures.

Our first notion was interesting in that we could reinforce the very strong, basic master plan geometries that emanated from Bill Pereira's master plan: the 'ring and spoke' plan. Most of UCI's buildings were designed as individual pavilions resting on sites along the way. We took the opportunity to make these buildings conform to but also help define the ring mall, anchoring the intersection between it and the spoke that led out from it perpendicularly.

We started with the Humanities Instructional Building, which followed the ring mall's curve to create a form to reinforce the intersection between the ring and spoke and then lead down the road to the spoke. Similarly, the Music and Media Building was located across a pedestrian bridge, but we used the abutments of the bridge to reinforce the spine. And the final building, the Fine Arts Building, was at the termination of this. Each building pays tribute to the campus's stated materials vocabulary.

I had a great working relationship with Jon Starr and Ken Lewis on this project. — DCM

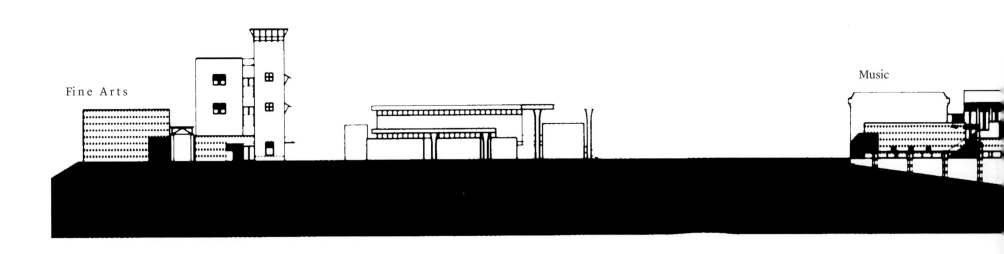

Fine Arts

Music

Music and Media Building

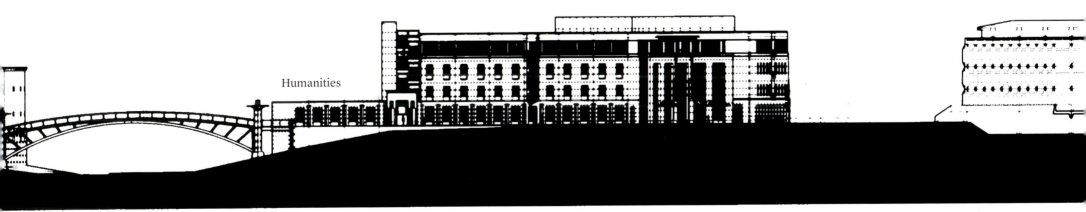

Humanities

PROJECT CREDITS

Client
University of California, Irvine

Designers
David C. Martin, Jon Starr

Project Director
Ken Lewis

**Structural Engineer/
MEP Engineer**
AC Martin

Humanities Instructional Building

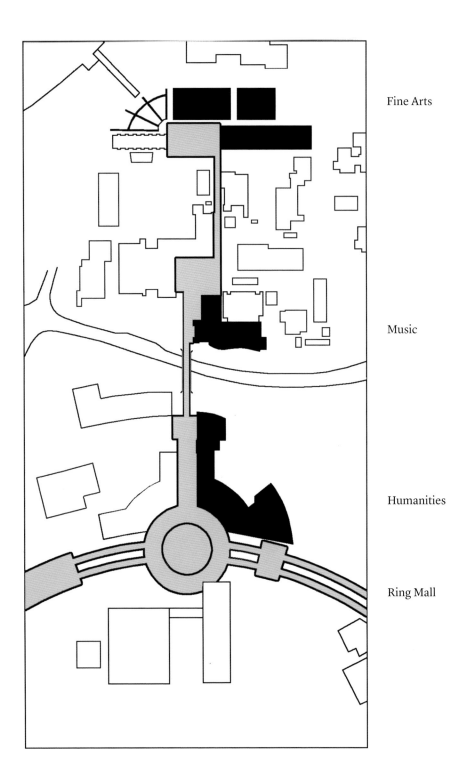

Fine Arts

Music

Humanities

Ring Mall

The spoke arrangement of the three buildings is anchored by UCI's established campus ring configuration, while a pedestrian bridge maintains a strong connection between them, extending campus pedestrian circulation.

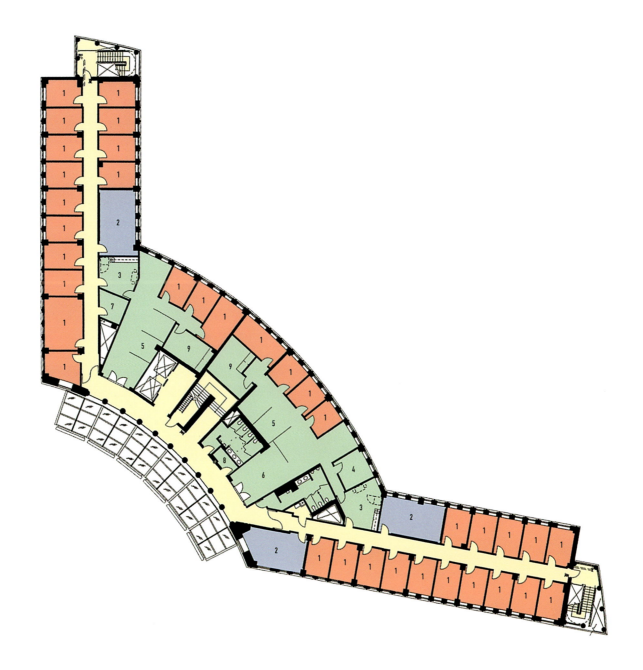

1. Office
2. Classroom
3. Workroom
4. Library
5. Clerical
6. Reception
7. Data
8. Electrical
9. Storage

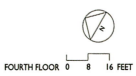

FOURTH FLOOR 0 8 16 FEET

Humanities Instructional Building

CALTRANS DISTRICT 3 HEADQUARTERS
Marysville, California 2009

This headquarters office building for the California Department of Transportation is a five-story structure featuring open offices for Caltrans' administration, design, and engineering studios. It includes a 200-seat auditorium, public service counters, teleconferencing facilities, and a cafeteria with outdoor seating.

The Caltrans Marysville Northern California Headquarters was a wonderful job for a very interesting and enjoyable client. This was a design-build competition where the team that could deliver the most interesting, quality building for the least amount of money would win the contract. We had a great working rapport with Turner Construction since we had worked together before.

The absolutely fascinating thing was that, to be able to price a proposal and ultimately win the competition, the team had to come together and conduct the majority of the design process upfront. Both Turner and AC Martin had experience working with Clark Pacific, a premier California precast firm known for high-quality work. We got the idea to create a long-span, precast concrete structure that was more or less brought in on trucks and assembled rapidly. The added benefit of this system was that the quality of concrete allowed for exposed construction.

It was a truly integrated team designing a high-performance, modular environment. We were focused on accurately estimating square footage so we wouldn't be over or under our target. It was excellent team spirit, and it worked. We arrived at a very competitive price with a very convincing scheme—and we won the job.

The goal of the project was to bring under one roof District 3's 800 employees, who were scattered throughout downtown Marysville in substandard buildings.

Charged with maintaining and operating the State's highway infrastructure, Caltrans' personnel are often faced with dangerous work, and they really need to protect one another. I could truly sense their esprit de corps. The leader of the corporate culture was a woman, unusual for the time. They often got together for company barbecues. And notably, District 3 owns a number of properties in the High Sierra for maintenance and storage purposes that also serve as campgrounds for the staff. We knew bringing this tight-knit group together in a multi-level building would only strengthen that bond. We focused on providing a space with good light and air while utilizing relatively large floor plates.

A prominent component of the building is the cavernous 4-story central space known as "The Canyon." Beginning on the second floor, it opens up to the light-filled interior, which is created by 115 linear feet of highly-reflective light louvers. No workspace is more than 37 feet from natural light.

We created a meandering atrium that connected the spaces not only two-dimensionally on one floor but also 3-dimensionally, so each floor had access to the others. Through this "canyon" we brought in a well-studied, natural south light where we examined its color temperature and the ways we could feed it through the building, saving the warm light and avoiding the cool light.

The Canyon also provides vertical visual communication, adding cohesiveness to the building's organization, as compared to traditionally stacked floors organized around a central core.

> The building was completed quickly and efficiently and is a truly integrated space filled with natural light, high ceilings, and nice materials. It's an absolutely first-class work environment for the District 3 staff.
>
> I thank Jamie Myer for his collaboration and Turner's Project Manager, Steven Schultz, for his dedication to this project's success. — DCM

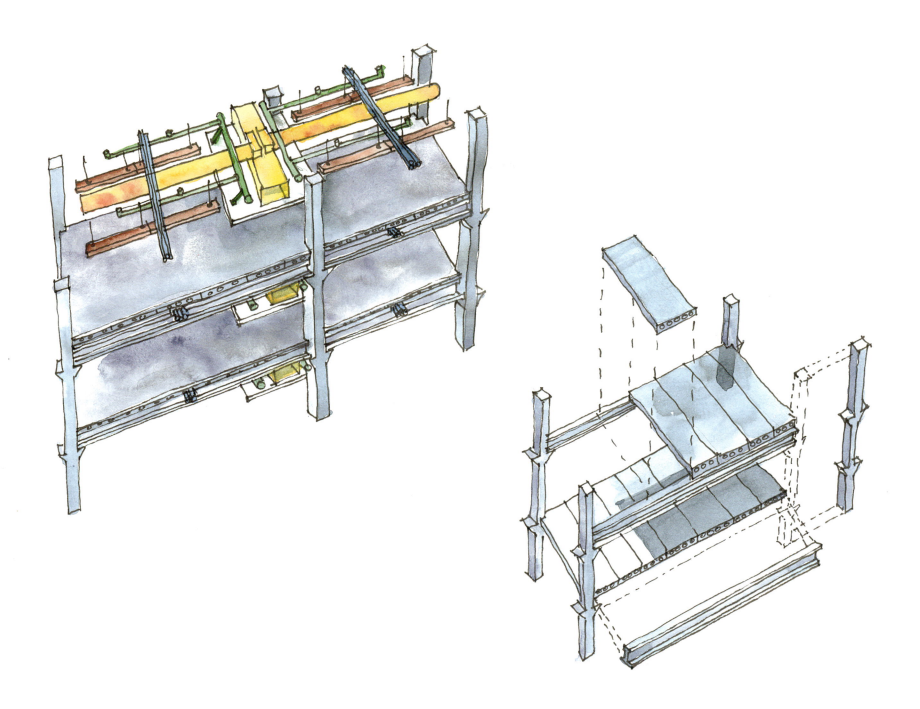

The building was delivered via design-build, utilizing a prefabricated building system.

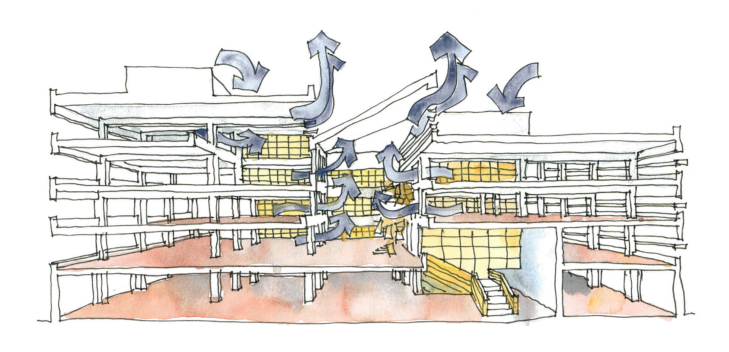

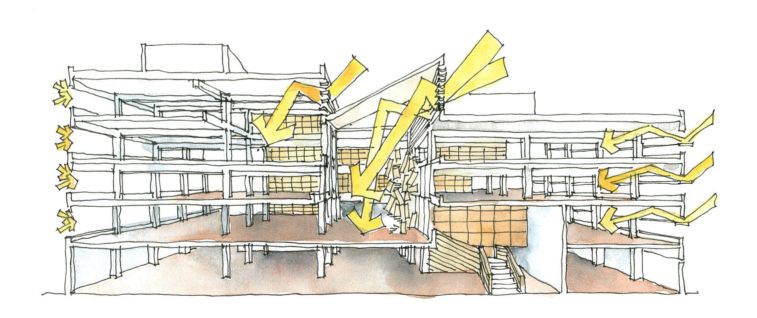

The MEP components were carefully studied to integrate with the design of the prefabricated building system. The blue arrows indicate natural ventilation and the yellow arrows indicate natural light.

PROJECT CREDITS

Client
California Department of Transportation

Designers
David C. Martin, Jamie Myer

Interior Designers
Susan Painter, Elizabeth Eshel, Clara Igonda (Clara Igonda Design)

Project Architect
George vanGilluwe

Project Managers
Rana Makarem, David Freedman

Chairman/CEO
Christopher C. Martin

Project Principal
Carey McLeod

Contractor
Turner Construction Company

Structural Engineer
Englekirk

MEP Engineer
Glumac

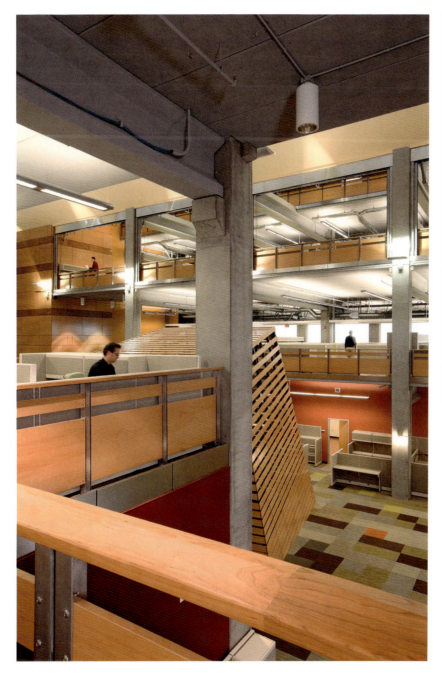

UNIVERSITY OF CALIFORNIA, DAVIS MATHEMATICAL SCIENCES BUILDING
Davis, California 2006

Located in the central core of the UC Davis campus, this 64,000-square-foot building provides office and research space for the Department of Mathematics, the Department of Statistics, the Center for Computational Science and Engineering, and the COSMOS (California State Summer School for Mathematics and Science) program. It includes offices, classrooms, conference rooms, a statistics lab, and a large seminar room for presentations and events.

> I'm very proud of this building. It had a modest budget, a constrained site, and a very specific interior program. By joining two sliding rectangles to form the building envelope and employing efficient circulation patterns both inside and out, we maximized the facility's use of the site.

> A modern, metal canopy serves as a sheltered walkway leading to the front entrance. The canopy formally announces the front door to the building, and keeps visitors from utilizing secondary doors for primary access. We always felt it was very important to address circulation paths and wayfinding early on in the planning process, especially when designing in the context of a large, established campus.

Important to the building's overall performance is its precast concrete building skin, which does an excellent job of adapting to the weather conditions of Central California. Its windows help mitigate heat gain while allowing 76% of the building access to outside views.

> I thank Campus Architect, Bob Strand, who was a very helpful client representative, and Paul Coleman for his valued design collaboration on this project. — DCM

PROJECT CREDITS

Client
University of California, Davis

Designers
David C. Martin, Paul Coleman

Project Architect
Bill Bussey

Project Director
Tom Emme

Contractor
Brown Construction

Structural Engineer
AC Martin

MEP Engineer
Capital Engineering Consultants

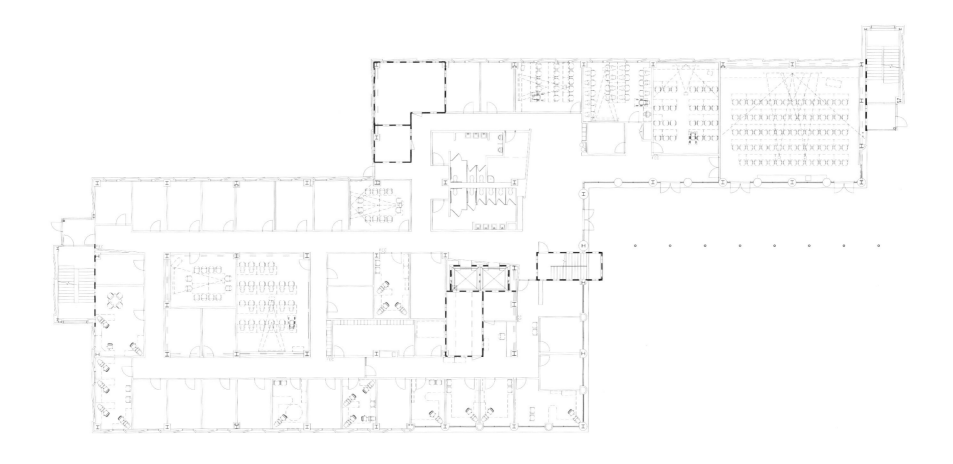

CALEPA HEADQUARTERS
Sacramento, California 2000

The project team had the tall order to furnish the California Environmental Protection Agency with a headquarters building that supported its mission: to restore, protect and enhance the environment to ensure public health, environmental quality, and economic vitality. The 25-story tower is located in Sacramento's urban core, just three blocks from the California State Capitol.

This was a design-build project with Turner Construction, where "best project" and "best value" were the criteria for getting the job. It was made very clear to the whole team that no additional monies would be provided for elements of the building earmarked for sustainability or the greening of the building. So every move we made to make the building efficient had to be given a tremendous value as a standard specification building rather than a building with sustainable features.

To do this, we started with the facility's most fundamental parts. First of all, it was to be located in central Sacramento along transit paths, not out in the suburbs, so the site itself was efficient. We then turned our attention to the major parts of the building that consumed energy. The first was the air conditioning system. Sacramento has a unique, diurnal climate. For most of the year, it is quite hot by day, but at night, it is very cool, caused by air flowing in from the Golden Gate area. We made the air conditioning system activate nightly to cool down the entire structure and create a cooling lag each morning. Interestingly, this was a very efficient way to deal with the climate. We also paid very close attention to the orientation of the building, the percentage of glass on each elevation, window sizes, and the like.

One of the joys of the project was that we were working with the designated CalEPA leadership responsible for the building criteria. They were very enthusiastic about creating a work style that was energy efficient, as were most people who worked for the agency.

So going through a series of scenarios and implementing many things that leaned more toward building efficiency than greening, we were able to achieve a building that was LEED Platinum certified that had the metrics of being one of the most efficient buildings in the country. In terms of its BTUs per square foot per year, it was maybe one of the best in the country for almost a period of 10 years.

The other notable part of this is, as part of our sustainability response, we also wanted to create a great public space for the City of Sacramento and the employees of CalEPA. The building's located across from a lovely park. It is on a classic 200' × 200' city block, as all blocks are in downtown Sacramento, so we created a corner plaza surrounded by the building and facing the park. You walk through a portal and enter this lovely public space with a beautiful sculpture by Beverly Pepper that includes a poem written by her daughter, Jorie Graham. We planted a grove of giant sequoias that now has quite wonderfully taken off. The daycare center is located here, so there is always this kind of delightful life on the plaza. The cafeteria faces out to the plaza as well, and there are lots of seats and other places for people to rest. As the public enters and exits the front lobby, marvelous people-watching opportunities occur.

All in all, as it's gone through the test of time, we think it's a very responsible public building for the State of California as well as the City of Sacramento.

TEN WAYS TO GREEN A BUILDING

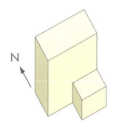

North/South Orientation: min. heat gain & max. daylighting

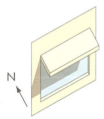

Overhangs on South Elevation: prevents solar gain at its worst

High Performance Glass: tuned to each elevation's exposure

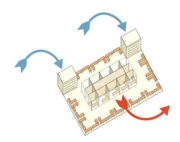

Abundant Fresh Air per Floor: diurnal use of microclimate to heat/cool

Open Offices on Perimeter: provides natural light to majority

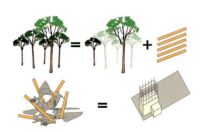

Sustainable Materials and Recycling of Construction Debris

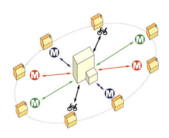

Central + Transit-friendly Site: contributes to energy savings and a morale boost

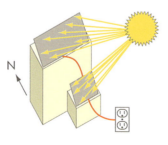

Extensive Photovoltaic Installation: provides building's own electricity

Planned Tenant Recycling Program: built-in systems improve usage rates

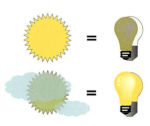

Computerized Lighting System: supplements daylight only as needed

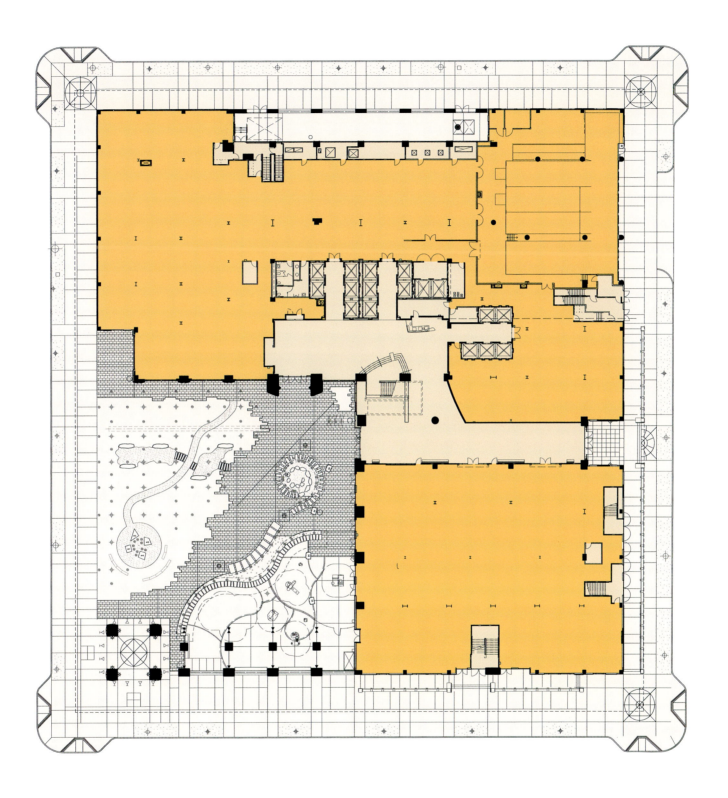

It was a key consideration to maximize community spaces throughout the site. A large outdoor plaza includes a childcare facility and faces a park across the street. There is also an outdoor cafe. These spaces work to enliven the grounds and keep the public engaged with the agency.

PROJECT CREDITS

Client
City of Sacramento/Thomas Properties Group, LLC (Public/Private Partnership)

Designers
David C. Martin, Ed Holakiewicz, Jon Starr, Tammy Jow

Interior Designers
IA Corporation, AC Martin (Gail Bouvrie-Public Lobby Interiors)

Project Architect
George vanGilluwe

Chairman/CEO
Christopher C. Martin

Project Principal
Carey McLeod

Project Directors
Fumio Konishi, Tom Emme

Contractor
Turner Construction Company

Structural Engineer
CBM Engineers

MEP Engineer
Levine Seegel Associates

For their significant contributions throughout the design process, I thank Theresa Parsley, Project Manager from CalEPA, and Tammy Jow and Ed Holakiewicz from AC Martin. —DCM

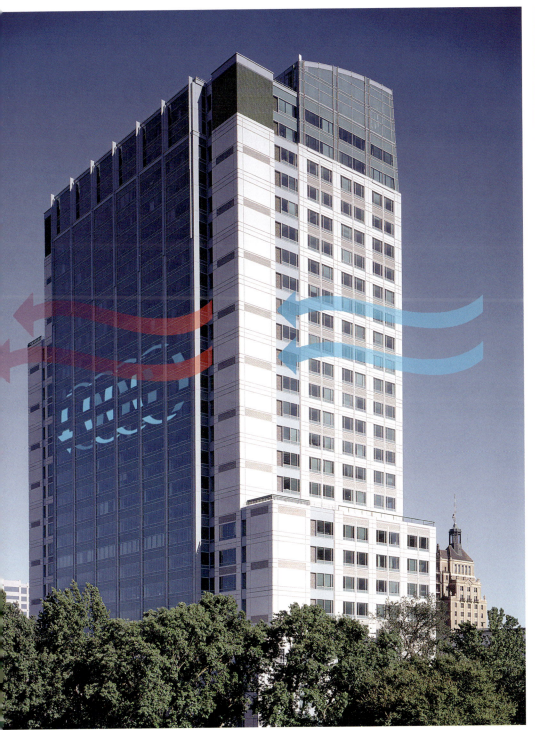

One of the nation's most efficient buildings, every floor of CalEPA takes advantage of natural air intake and exhaust guided by Sacramento's hot days and cold nights.

SPRINGLEAF TOWER
Singapore, 2002

The 37-story Springleaf Tower is located on a very restricted site in Singapore's central business district, surrounded by high-rises.

This was a wonderful opportunity to design a highly mixed-use building in the exciting urban core of a premier Asian city. The building is a mix of residential, office, retail, and parking. It even has a gas station in it.

I came to the project with the typical Western mindset of office space being a percentage of net-to-gross, the height of the building being dictated by the efficiency of the elevators, and so on. But I was quickly presented with an entirely different set of values, including the practice of feng shui and the significance of numerology, as we worked toward a design solution. It was a fabulous learning experience for me.

The tower is a combination of both round and rectangular forms, is clad in a highly-articulated stainless steel curtain wall with a granite base, and is crowned with a lantern that glows dramatically on the evening skyline. Its two uppermost floors contain executive penthouse apartments where tenants can house visiting clients. A five-story podium features a grand lobby with glass walls overseeing a tropical garden, a conference center that opens onto a roof garden, parking for 200 cars, and a lower-level link to the adjacent subway station.

To maximize lease depths, make the most efficient use of narrow floor plates, and capitalize on significant but limited views, the elevator core is offset to the rear of the site. Raised floors allow flexibility in accommodating telecommunications and computer equipment in the 400,000-square-foot building.

I thank Bill Bussey for his dedication to this project. — DCM

PROJECT CREDITS

Client
Springleaf

Designers
David C. Martin, Ed Holakiewicz

Project Architect
Bill Bussey

Contractor
Yangnam Holdings

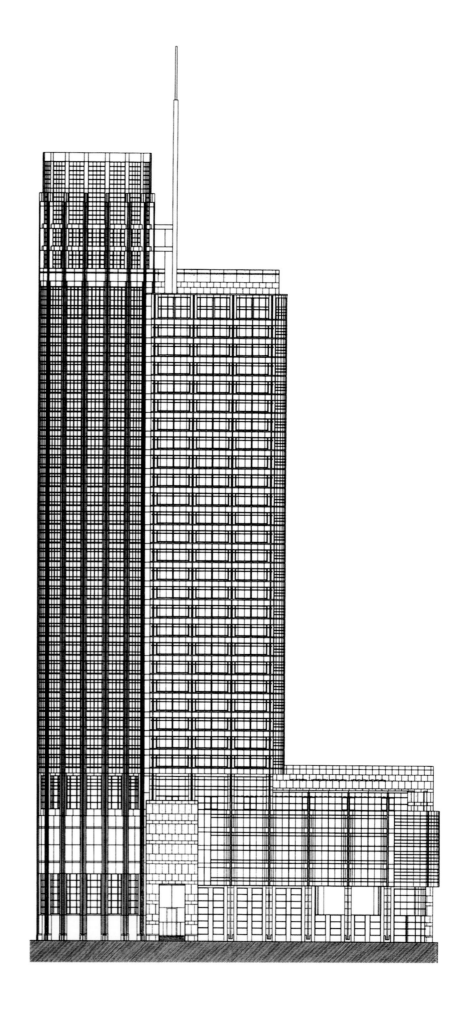

UNIVERSITY OF SOUTHERN CALIFORNIA
RONALD TUTOR CAMPUS CENTER

Los Angeles, California 2010

David's interest in town planning, and his exploration of public spaces around the world, is evident at his alma mater, the University of Southern California. Master planned during the 1920s and 1930s, the school was strictly a city campus lacking a core for interactive student life. It was completely car-centric, with blocks of buildings surrounded by roads and parallel parking.

Over the years, the campus has grown and evolved into a quasi-city, and it now has a bona fide gathering place in the Ronald Tutor Campus Center. At its center is a piazza designed to adhere to the principles of a good public place. It includes thoughtful areas dedicated to sun and shade, places to sit, food service, and space for interesting activities. It is a classic, urban outdoor environment.

The big idea here was surely to create a heart and soul of the USC campus, which didn't exist beforehand. We competed for this job with a number of good firms, several from the East Coast, and we found out later we were the only ones to suggest that this become the campus space in a significant way. I think the others all understood the program to mean creating a grand, large building. We perceived it to mean creating a grand, large space.

All the ingredients were there to introduce to the campus a marvelous, Southern California outdoor space filled with activity. This was to become the central food facility for the campus, the campus store, the Admission Center, the Alumni Center, the president's dining room, and much more. Orienting all of these functions generally toward this campus space would add to the overall vibrancy of the facility.

Two existing buildings formed two of the perimeter walls, so all we had to do was add an L-shaped building to create a marvelous rectangular plaza. We were also able to establish new pathways leading to other quadrants of the campus, to ensure that this major public space always remains at a strong crossroads.

Years after completion, every time I walk through, it's just filled with people. It's become the meeting place on campus.

The Campus Center serves as USC's "town hall," providing offices, lounges, entertainment facilities, dining and retail areas, conference and multi-purpose rooms, and a variety of food-service venues. Its exterior is a modern interpretation of Romanesque architecture, which complements the surrounding campus context.

Tammy Jow (USC '95) helped me (USC '66) design something truly special for our alma mater. Patrick Bailey, USC's Senior Associate Dean of Students, and Jason Cruz, USC's Project Coordinator, were excellent client representatives. Tutor Center would not be the success it is without their contributions. —DCM

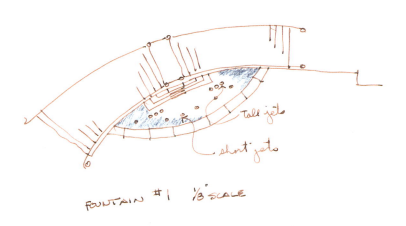

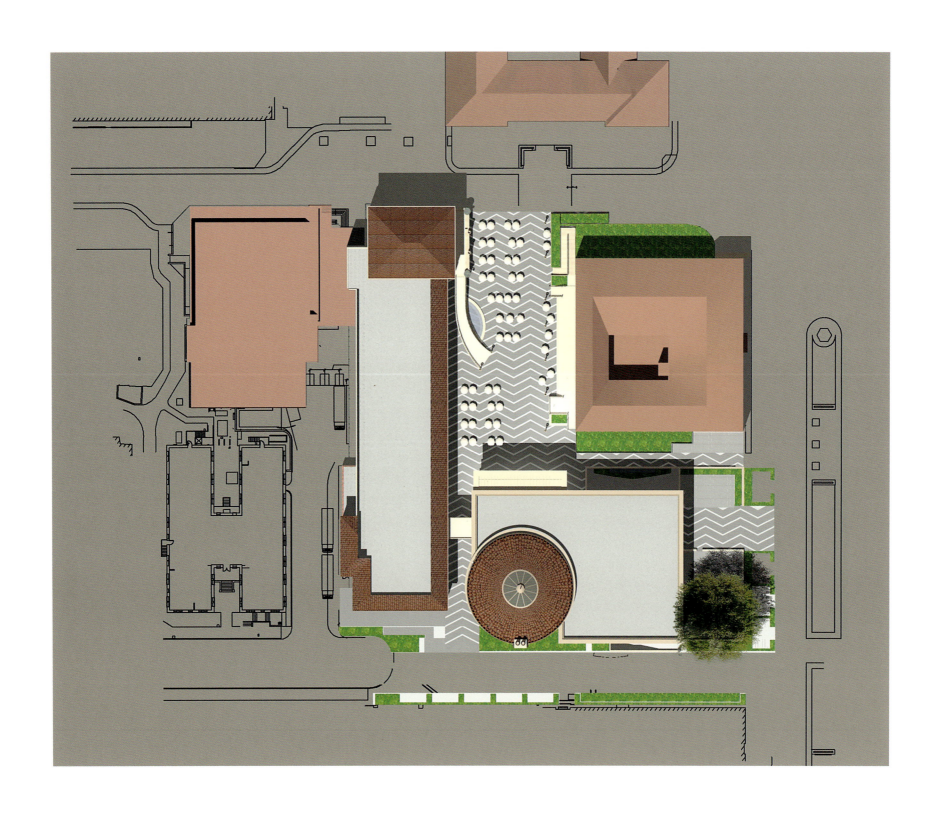

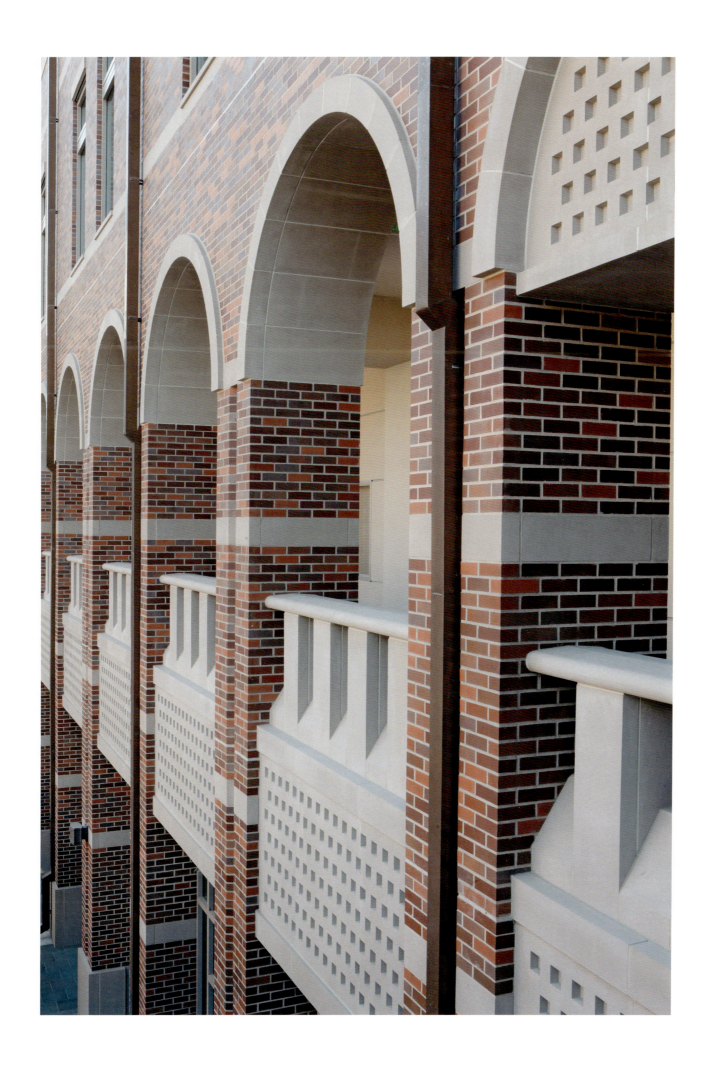

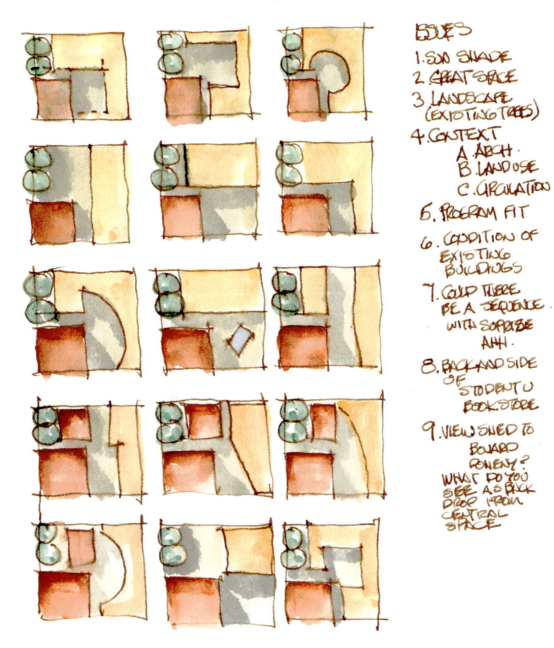

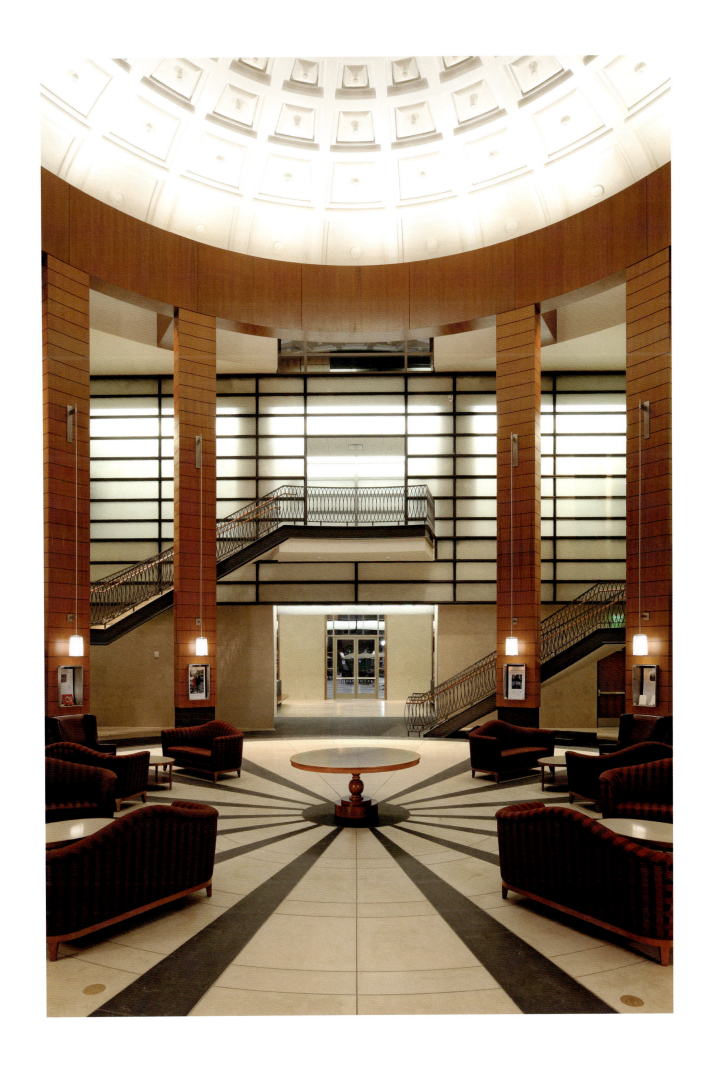

PROJECT CREDITS

Client
University of Southern California

Designers
David C. Martin, Tammy Jow,
Eun Gu Lee

Interior Designers
Christopher King, Grit Pasker

Project Architect
George vanGilluwe

Project Director
Robert R. Murrin

Contractor
Tutor-Saliba Corporation

Structural Engineer
Saiful Bouquet

MEP Engineer
Glumac

FLINTRIDGE PREPARATORY SCHOOL
RANDALL PERFORMING ARTS CENTER
La Cañada Flintridge, California 2000

The Randall Performing Arts Center is a supportive and dynamic environment where students explore the world of artistic performance in the areas of dance, drama, vocal and instrumental music, and stage technology.

This is a humble, simple structure where the performing arts functions are joined together in a two-story, L-shaped building. The site is located at the foot of a hill. This provided an opportunity to form a semi-sheltered, central, open-space amphitheater along the hillside, creating an outdoor meeting space for the school's various disciplines. We also provided an additional pathway for students to use as a pass-through to the athletic fields and facilities beyond.

The 10,000-square-foot facility includes an 80-seat black box theater, dance studio, music and dance rehearsal space, dressing rooms, and storage, all at ground level, with classrooms located on the second floor. A metal canopy and outdoor catwalk connect the upper floor to stadium-style steps for audience seating.

Thank you to Ines Gomez-Chessum for her design collaboration on this project. — DCM

PROJECT CREDITS

Client
Flintridge Preparatory School

Designers
David C. Martin,
Ines Gomez-Chessum

Project Principal
Robert R. Murrin

Contractor
Dumark Corporation

**Structural Engineer/
MEP Engineer**
AC Martin

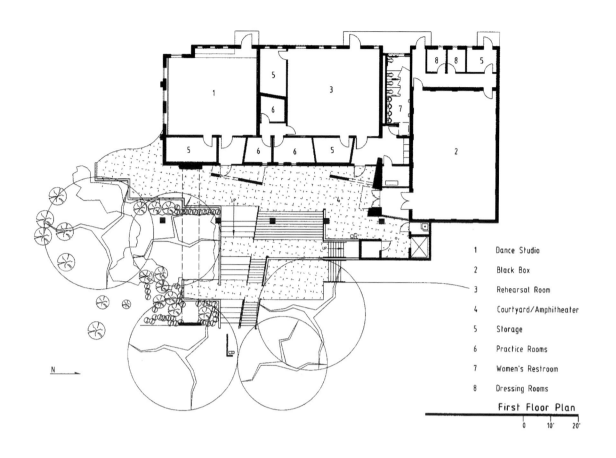

1	Dance Studio
2	Black Box
3	Rehearsal Room
4	Courtyard/Amphitheater
5	Storage
6	Practice Rooms
7	Women's Restroom
8	Dressing Rooms

First Floor Plan

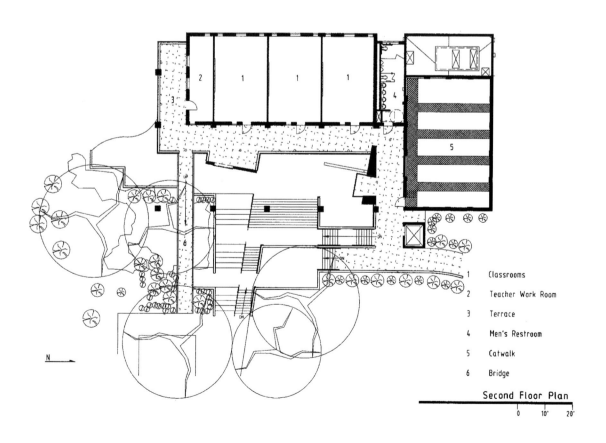

1	Classrooms
2	Teacher Work Room
3	Terrace
4	Men's Restroom
5	Catwalk
6	Bridge

Second Floor Plan

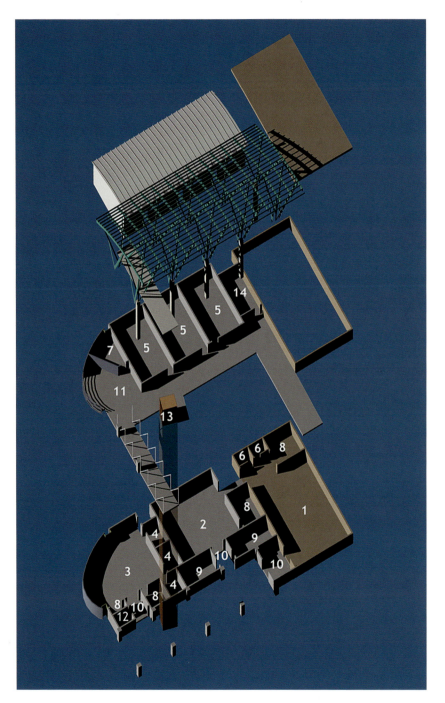

1   Black Box Theater
2   Dance Studio / Drama
3   Music Room
4   Practice Room
5   Seminar Room
6   Dressing Room
7   Teacher Workroom / Electronic Music Lab
8   Storage
9   Toilet
10 Vestibule
11 Observation Deck
12 Elevator Equipment Room
13 Elevator
14 HVAC Equipment Room

RUSTIC CANYON RESIDENCE
Santa Monica, California 1994– Present

David's family home occupies a 2.5-acre hillside site in a secluded section of Santa Monica.

We lived on the property for many years before we started construction. The site had a very run-down house on it that we made habitable until we could create the drawings and build the new house around the old one (which we would later demolish).

During those early days, there were several things we came to realize about the site that became the basis of our plan. First, we discovered a 50-year-old road leading from the top of the hill above in Pacific Palisades, descending across our property, and terminating at Rustic Creek at the base of our lot. It was dedicated to the ranchers, to move their cows from grazing in the upper pastures to watering down in the creek. And there were trees planted along that route, which created a great arch on one side of the site. Also, the clearing surrounding the existing house was flat, with the mature landscape nearly forming a circle around it, open to the sky.

Out of these conditions came our master plan of creating a house that was curved and built into the hillside, with a plaza and small structures around it. This expanded the notion of what I've always been interested in: creating a village where one could walk from structure to structure throughout the activities of the day. This also allowed us to build out these structures over a period of time, since we couldn't afford to construct the whole complex at once.

The crescent-shaped house is a modern interpretation of classical shapes and forms: spheres, cylinders, cubes, pyramids, and barrel vaults. River rock and concrete make up the lower portion of the structure, leading to a massive, glazed entry door. A double-height, barrel-vaulted grand room, with adjacent salon, dining, library, and music spaces, features furnishings David has designed, as well as those selected by French interior designer, Andrée Putman, and art is everywhere. Upstairs are bedrooms and generous dressing areas. A separate apartment structure dedicated to visiting family is connected to the main house by a wisteria-covered walkway.

A studio, garages, a lap pool with pool house, an office, and a gymnasium ring the plaza. A sculptural bridge spans the property's arroyo, designed and constructed using the latest advancements in robotic design. Traversing the bridge is part of a series of experiences fundamental to the Rustic Canyon residence. Everything is connected via pathways within the wooded hillside. Amphitheaters provide intimate settings for parties and live performances. A limonaia and olive grove allude to the family's attachments to Italy and enhance the rural feel of the location.

After over 25 years, the Martins' Rustic Canyon residence continues to be a work in progress.

From the house's beginnings, John Uniack has had a major design impact on the property, keeping his eye on the details and seeing projects through from design concept to completion. Bruce Brown was our on-site contractor for many years. Scott Mitchell was the driving force behind the bridge's design and off-site robotic assembly. Tammy Jow was responsible for the addition of the pool house. My thanks go to all for their help in making this home such a joy for Mary and me, our family, and our friends. — DCM

PROJECT CREDITS

Client
David C. Martin
and Mary Klaus Martin

Designers
David C. Martin, John Uniack,
Scott Mitchell, Tammy Jow

Contractors
Bovee Construction,
Brown Ósvaldsson, Inc.

Key Subcontractors
High Class Welding, Inc., DEC
Fabricators, Inc., Janisse & Son, Inc.

Structural Engineer
Nabih Youssef & Associates

MEP Engineer
AC Martin

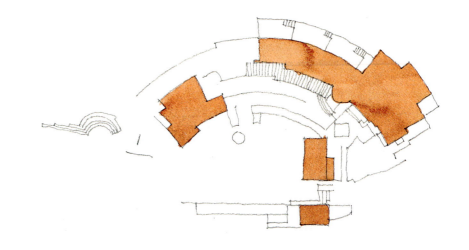

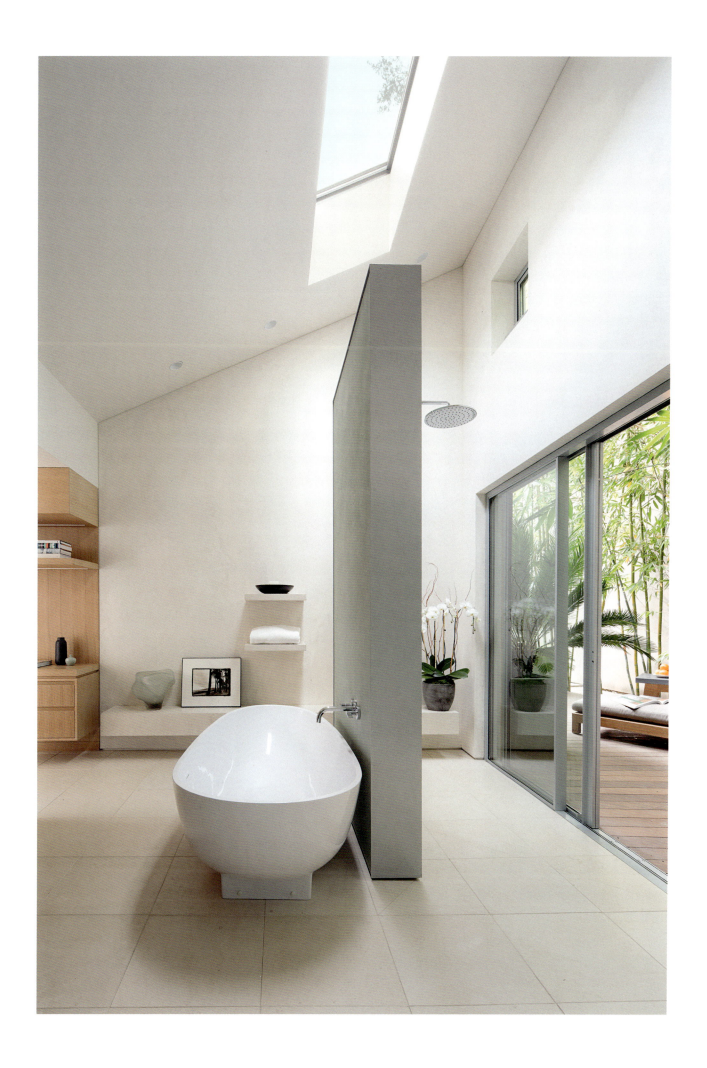

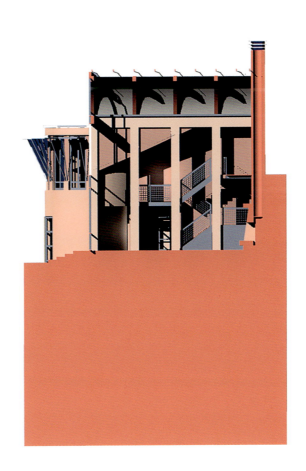

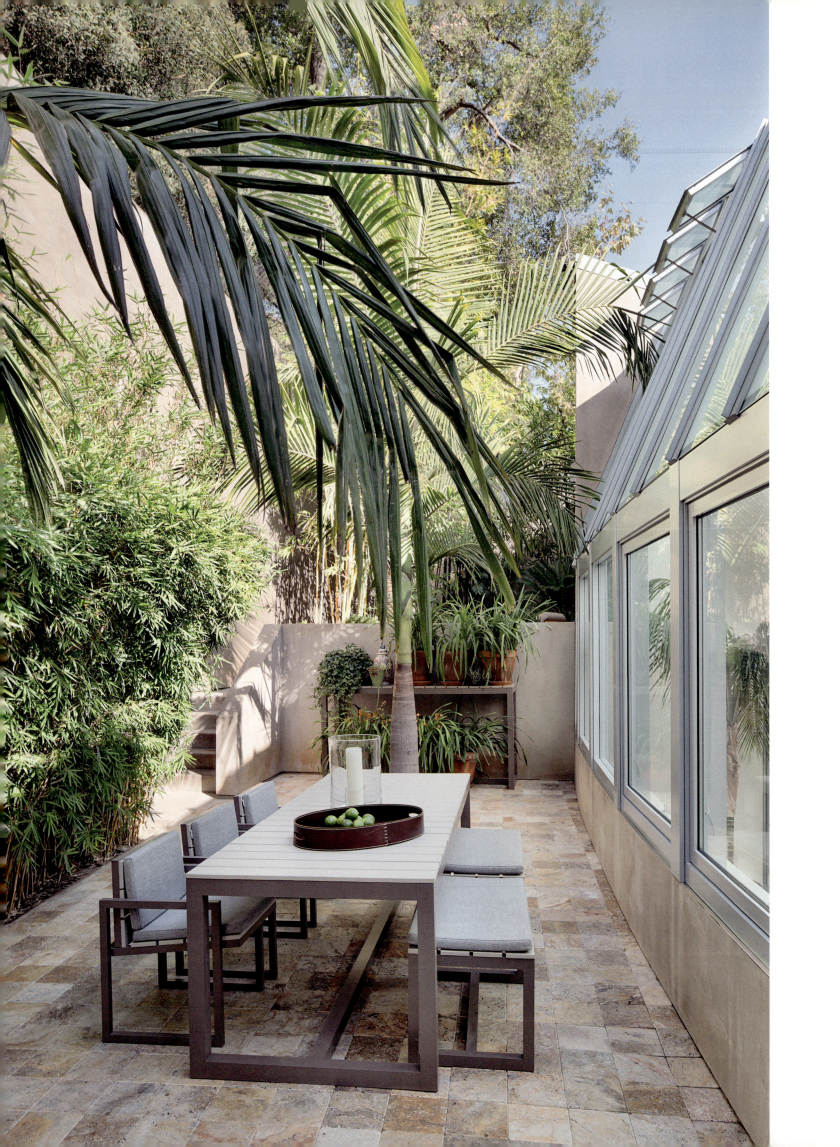

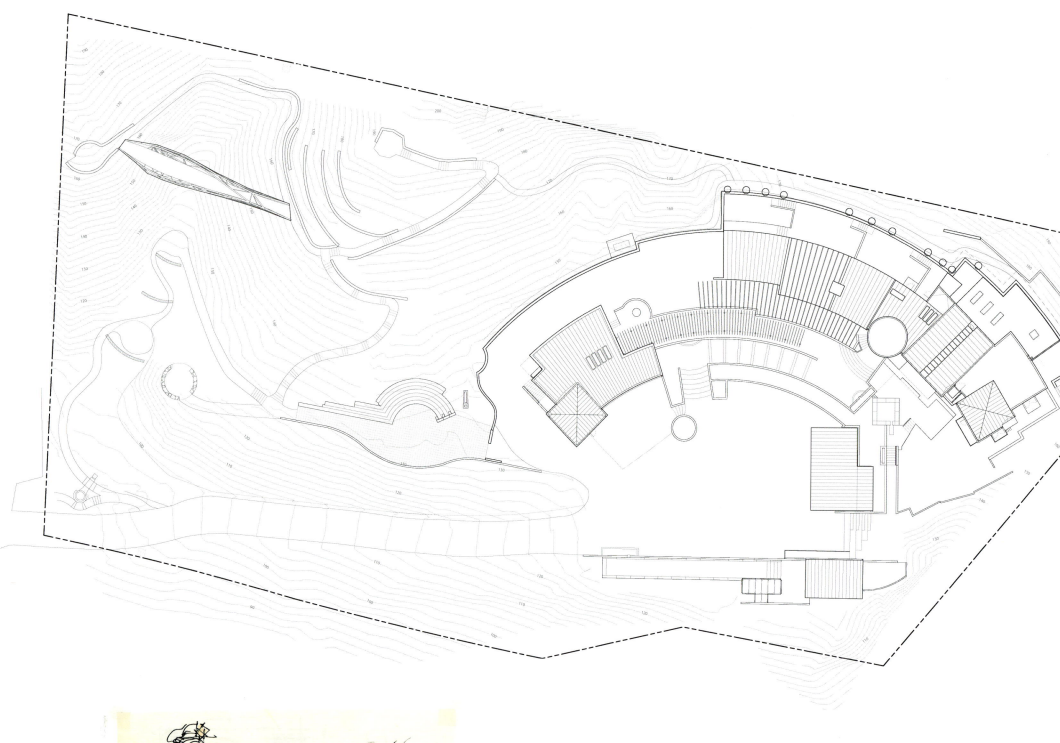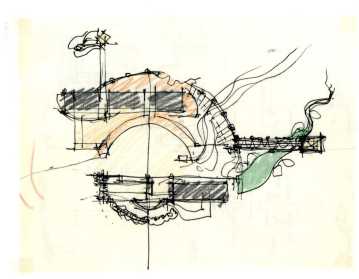

PADRE SERRA PARISH
Camarillo, California 1995

In 1910, David's grandfather designed the City of Camarillo's first Catholic church—St. Mary Magdalen—so it was a special honor for David to make his own design contribution to the community more than eight decades later.

The project's master plan included the main worship sanctuary with support areas, chapel, classrooms and offices, parochial school, daycare facility, multi-purpose building, rectory, and play fields for the school.

Padre Serra was the first church I had ever designed. I was about 15 years into my career, and for the most part, I was designing office buildings. But there was a market change, and commercial building was at a lull.

My cousin, Bud Daily, asked if I would get involved with designing a Catholic church in Camarillo, and I said I would be delighted. My grandfather and his brother, Emmet, had designed many, many Catholic churches around the Southwest, as far away as Arizona and throughout California, so this was my first opportunity to sit within the family tradition.

It's interesting to note that my uncle was a very devout and conservative Catholic, while the Cardinal at the time, Roger Mahony, was a liberal Catholic. They had previously had intense conversations about the two points of view within the Church, and the Cardinal wanted to be sure that kind of dialogue would not get in the way of the design process. So he suggested I attend a 3-day seminar put on by a marvelous lady about Catholic traditions.

This was during the time that the Church was introducing a new liturgy, and new forms were being explored. This was actually quite phenomenal because as one studies the great cathedrals, particularly from the Renaissance period, you begin to understand a real rationale for all kinds of different reflections of the form and what ritual the form of these churches might be taking. I really enjoyed the seminar, and the design of the church did end up being an altar-in-the-round, promoting a sense of congregation, as compared to an inwardly-focused, individual religious experience.

This project was a wonderful undertaking thanks to the Parish's pastor, Father Liam Kidney. He was a real character—a young Irishman who taught me a lot. We visited different churches up and down the state, and he would show me the ingredients and nuances of designing a church, not only from a ritual standpoint but from the technical side, involving acoustics and ergonomics and issues that happen when large numbers of people gather.

In that process, I also came to realize that a church is not just a big, lofty interior space, but that the truly great churches have a sense of pageantry, a sense of journey to them; that the religious experience starts as one arrives on the church grounds, through a courtyard or a foyer. This is the point where fellow parishioners meet, and the priest welcomes everyone. It becomes a ritual and even a festival. One goes through the front door, the narthex, the nave, and with this procession, experiences a whole sequence of marvels, amounting to much more than merely entering into a large, dimly-lit, dramatic space.

It was an unusual design situation for me to be in since I had spent so many years working on the metrics for office buildings. I was so focused on gross-to-net and how cheaply we could do this and that. One day, Father Kidney said to me, 'David, I've got 5 million bucks. How much spirituality can I get for 5 million bucks?' That was such an interesting and provocative thought. I loved it because this is why I became an architect—to be able to express things that are beyond the obvious but have more to do with the depth of the experience.

David's design of the church complex is a modern adaptation of the California Mission style. A series of tree-lined drives lead to and from a ceremonial auto court located at the entrance to a central courtyard. The courtyard, shaded by California pepper trees and with an inviting fountain, functions as a gathering space before and after worship and for parish events.

The courtyard leads directly to the hall of worship, which is octagonal in shape. Inside, the altar rests in the center of the space, surrounded by individual chairs rather than pews, putting greater emphasis on the congregation. Its high ceiling is comprised of large, exposed wood beams, providing warmth and intimacy.

A 2000 reader's poll by Los Angeles Lay Catholic Mission magazine ranked Padre Serra Parish Church among the top ten best churches in the archdiocese for its architecture, citing its "complete 'village' concept" and "integrity," among other notable qualities.

I thank Father Liam Kidney, who was a fabulous teacher in the basics of church design, and Ed Holakiewicz of AC Martin, who provided expert design collaboration. — DCM

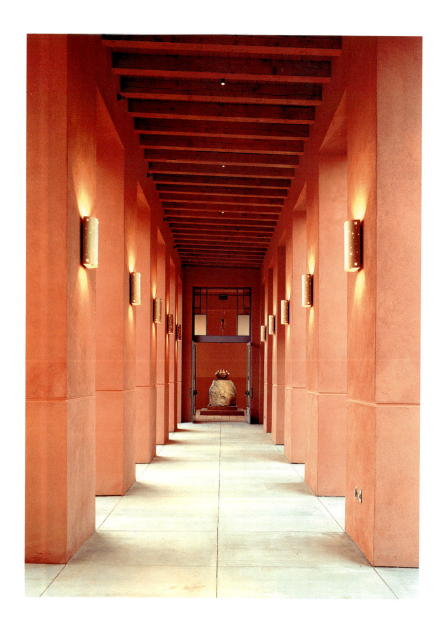

PROJECT CREDITS

Client
Archdiocese of Los Angeles

Designers
David C. Martin, Ed Holakiewicz

Landscape Architect
Susan Van Atta (Van Atta Associates, Inc.)

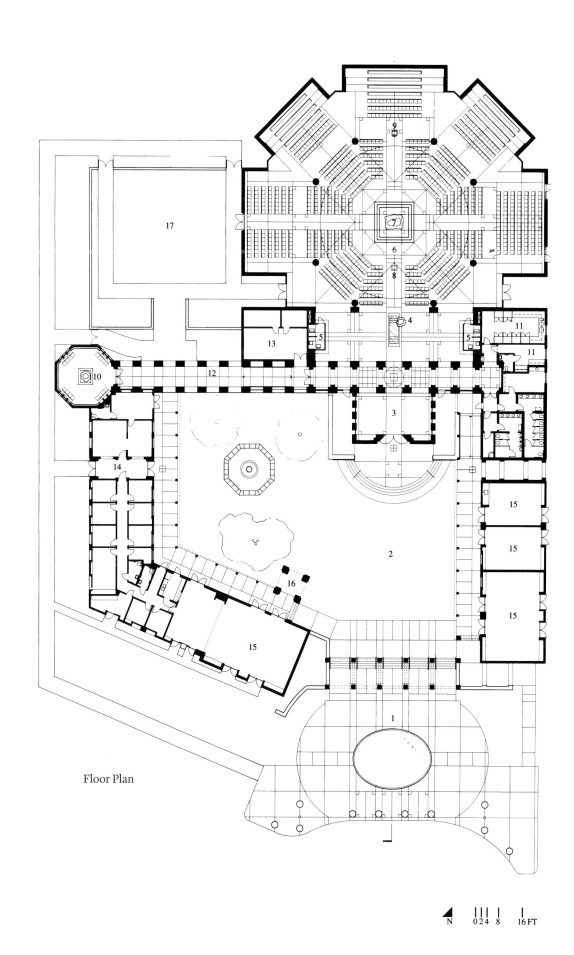

Floor Plan

1. Entrance Plaza
2. Courtyard
3. Narthex
4. Baptismal Font
5. Reconciliation Room
6. Sanctuary
7. Altar
8. Presider's Chair
9. Ambo
10. Reservation Chapel
11. Sacristy
12. Processional Arcade
13. Storage
14. Parish Offices
15. Classroom
16. Bell Tower
17. Worship Garden

INSPIR
INSPIR

ATION
ATION

INSPIRATION

It could be that design inspiration is not what it seems. For me, inspiration comes from architecture that may not be an architect's best work, world-renowned, or sophisticated in others' eyes, but for some reason, it leaves its mark on me.

One example is the souk Jemaa el-Fnaa in Marrakesh. I would send any aspiring architect there to decipher what's going on. It's one of the world's most magical places, with caravans of exotic goods, food, entertainment, the wonderful Ben Youssef Madrasa in the middle of the bazaar, and a massive labyrinth of shops just off the main square.

It could be that inspiration corresponds to what you are looking for. Perhaps context and timing are ingredients. It could be it's the quest for a message you are looking to receive.

For me to be truly inspired, it must be a memorable life-changing event. I want to take the experience, the idea, away with me. I want to record it in writing, take photos, do drawings, and even make a model of the place, so I can in some way possess this phenomenon, this new knowledge.

Architectural experiences that have (in a good way) shaken my beliefs can be described as events. Sometimes these events happen by accident. Sometimes they are the result of a drawn-out study, leading to a literal pilgrimage of discovery. I once discovered a Baroque-era Jesuit church while coming around a corner on my motorcycle. I was far into the desert, and this church was barely on a map, seemingly on no one's radar. Other times, such as my first visit to Pueblo Bonito in Chaco Canyon, New Mexico, the long journey happened because years earlier, my professor, Ralph Knowles, gave a lecture on the rationale for its form. I had similar experiences with the Golden Temple of Amritsar in India and the Valley of the Kings in Egypt. One thing I can verify, sometimes consciously, but often unconsciously—these events come up as references in the design process. These experiences become part of who you are. They are neatly tucked up in your mind, ready to come out at the appropriate moment. When you put your whole effort into the creative process, the things that you value flow right onto the paper in front of you.

One of the world's great houses. It's as if every wall, floor, and ceiling were organized for color and composition in a 2-dimensional manner, then pieced together to make the house.

CASA LUIS BARRAGÁN
Mexico City, Mexico

JEMAA EL-FNAA
Marrakesh, Morocco

On-site sketch of Jemaa el-Fnaa central square, an extremely vibrant urban space that defies all preconceptions about proper urban design. The exotic character of the sounds, smells, colors, and goods add to the human interaction that is happening at an intense level.

THE PYRES OF VARANASI
Varanasi, India

Majestic architecture as a backdrop
to the drama of life and death.

THE GOLDEN TEMPLE
Amritsar, India

The plan for the Golden Temple of Amritsar is an elemental composition: a square perimeter of marble surrounding a large pool with a golden temple in the center. Theatrical, powerful, and iconic.

PUEBLO BONITO
Chaco Canyon, New Mexico

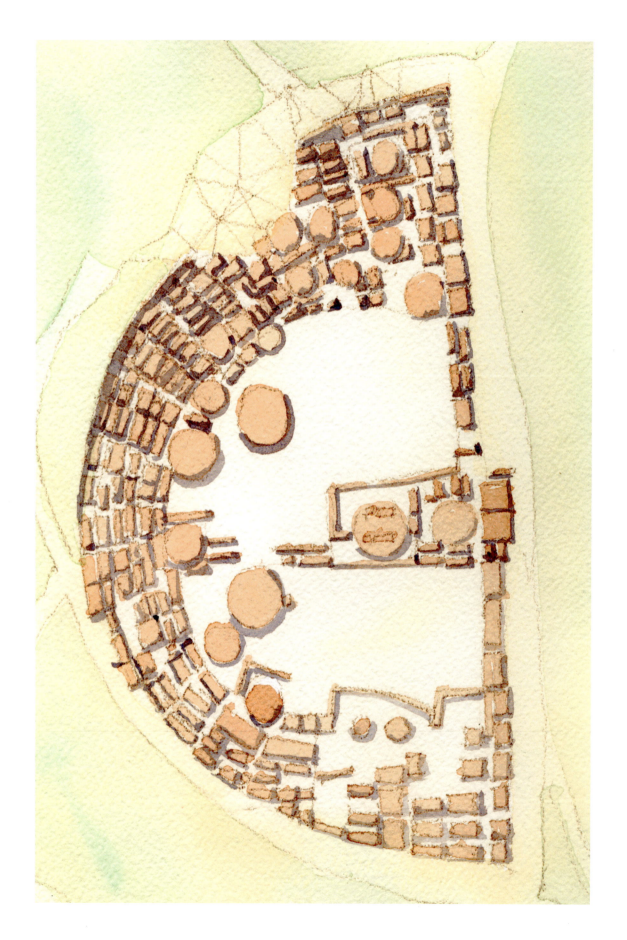

This is perhaps the greatest pre-Columbian structure in North America. I first learned of it through architect Ralph Knowles in his lectures on design with nature at the USC School of Architecture.

FALLINGWATER

Mill Run, Pennsylvania

To me, this design by Frank Lloyd Wright is the greatest house in America.

V. C. MORRIS GIFT SHOP
San Francisco, California

I grew up with modern architecture all around me,
but when I visited Frank Lloyd Wright's Morris Gift Shop,
I knew this was something entirely different.

ROCKEFELLER CENTER
New York, New York

America's great, "Big City" urban space. Art, composition, entertainment, and open space—all the ingredients are there.

GUANAJUATO

Guanajuato , Mexico

I first heard about Guanajuato from Charles Moore, who described it as his favorite city in the world. When Mary and I first visited, unbeknownst to us, it happened to be the Feast of Our Lady of Guadalupe. We joined the procession to visit the basilica on the hilltop above the main street. People came from miles around to join in the rituals, festivals, and joy of life.

BRADBURY BUILDING
Los Angeles, California

This is a wonderful architectural surprise and the oldest commercial building still standing in the central city. It was perfectly natural for it to become home to many of the characters in Ridley Scott's colossal film, *Blade Runner*.

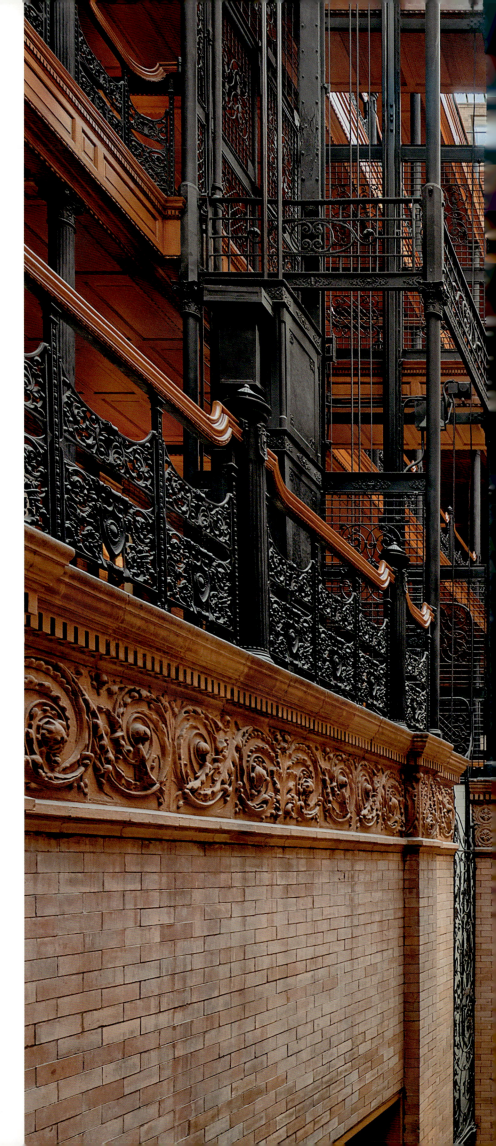

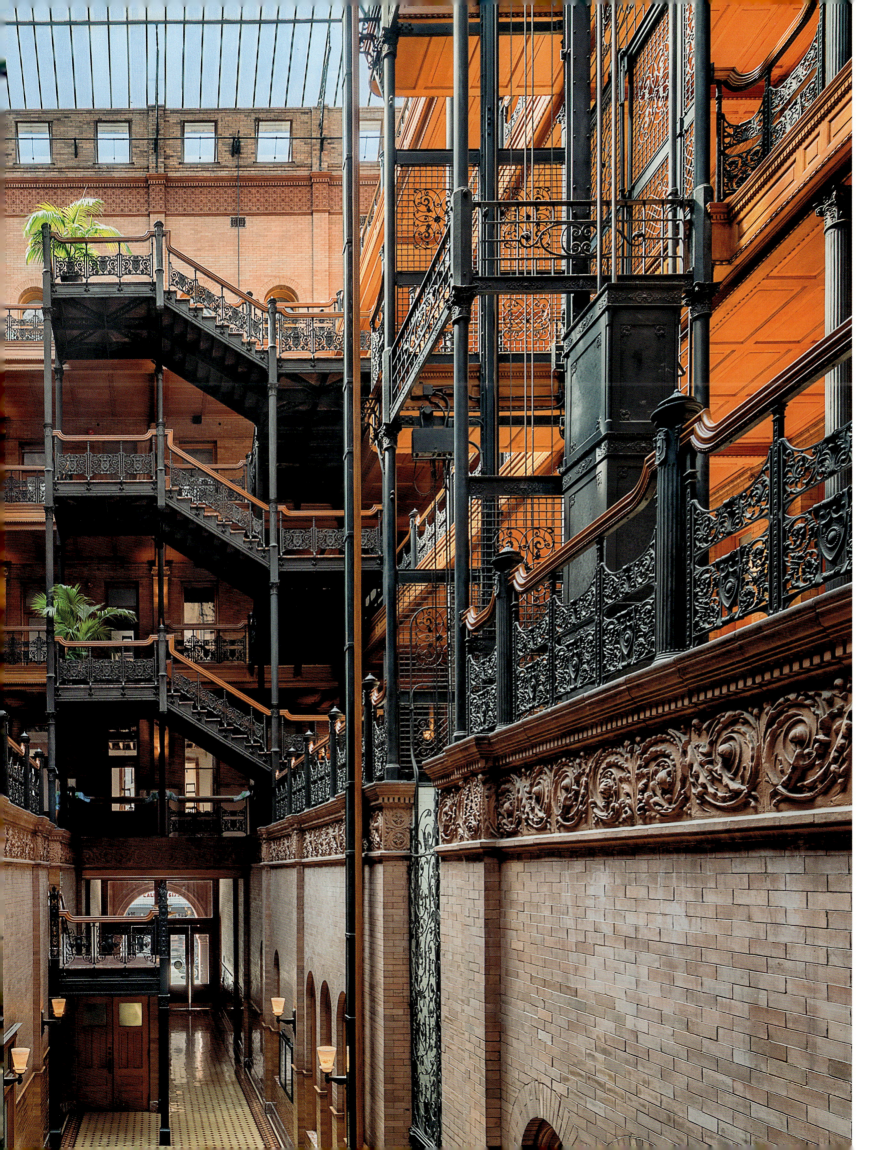

UNB
W

ORK

OREGON STATE UNIVERSITY STUDENT CENTER

A student center for Oregon State including student offices, classrooms, and food center. High priority was given to sustainable communal space and natural light. Activities were organized to encourage interaction and collegiality among faculty, staff, and the student body.

SAN JOAQUIN COUNTY ADMINISTRATION BUILDING

Our proposal for this design-build competition acknowledged a forward-thinking community with deep respect for their area's existing historic core. The program called for San Joaquin County departmental offices and a strong public interface component.

LAX CONSOLIDATED RENT-A-CAR (CONRAC) FACILITY

We designed this facility for a large plot of land owned by Los Angeles World Airports. The site is located adjacent to the 405 Freeway, leading into the airport. The goal was to congregate major rental car agencies into a single facility, connecting to the central core of the airport and common transit links, allowing passengers and baggage to flow in and out more easily.

Our design sited the facility on top of a large, specially-constructed parking structure surrounded by earth, in a park-like environment. The open-air concept was energy-efficient, taking advantage of the mild Southern California weather, with its constant, gentle sea breezes that grace the airport area.

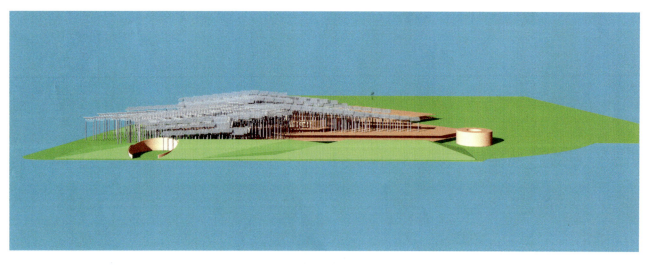

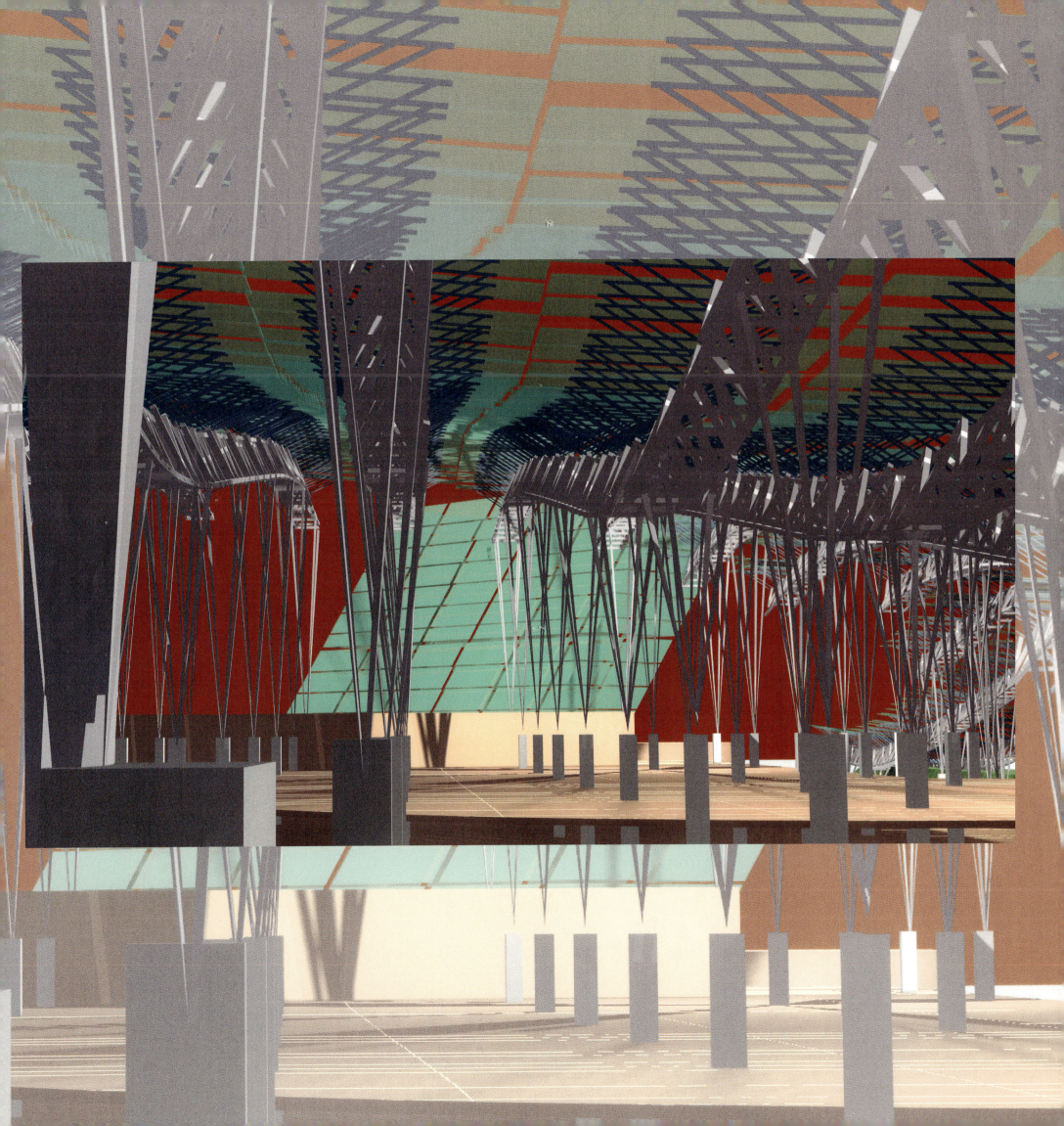

TEMECULA RESORT AND SPA

This was a concept for a resort-spa complex sited in the middle of the Temecula Valley wine region. The program included a conference center, restaurant, spa, tennis center, pool, and hotel suites, all within a working vineyard, forming an elegant luxury destination resort in a rural part of Southern California.

BAKERSFIELD FEDERAL COURTHOUSE

We entered this design-build competition for a new courthouse sited along a small lake in a central Bakersfield park. Our scheme featured a strong solar protection component, as well as design elements related to the scale and history of the park.

VENTURA HISTORY MUSEUM

We won this competition to expand an existing, small, county history museum designed by AC Martin in the '70s, but the project was never realized. The building sits in the center of the historic core of Ventura, adjacent to Mission San Buenaventura. The original scheme was in the Spanish Mediterranean style. This new proposal would have added about 30,000 square feet for a total area of approximately 55,000 square feet. The scheme incorporated wood trelliswork with natural stone boulders in keeping with the historic Mission. The vertical central hall gave the museum a strong community presence. The collections and displays reflected the area's rich agricultural past, as well as its more recent beach and surf-oriented history.

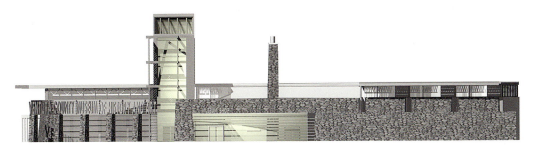

NORTH ELEVATION

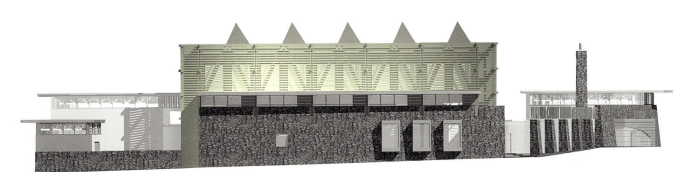

EAST ELEVATION

205

LAUSD 17TH AND GRAND HIGH SCHOOL

This project involved the conversion of an under-utilized parking structure at 17th Street and Grand Avenue in Los Angeles to form a creative high school for the Los Angeles Unified School District. Our design included classrooms surrounding a central, naturally lit, open space, with food services and athletics on the roof.

This conversion scheme became quite attractive because of its central location, land cost, structural cost, and speed of construction. It also led to an unconventional but rich solution for community and student interaction in a dynamic learning environment.

MATTEL DESIGN CENTER

We designed a 250,000-square-foot research and development center to be located adjacent to Mattel's headquarters. It featured flexible, open, and collegial space where adjacencies encouraged interaction and creativity. Programmatic requirements called for strong connectivity among the design staff of the various divisions of the company, including such identifiable brands as Barbie, Hot Wheels, and G.I. Joe. North-facing skylights were included to bring daylight into the central open space.

CHAPMAN UNIVERSITY
ANACONDA STUDENT HOUSING

This scheme took an existing, historic, truss warehouse owned by Chapman University and introduced modular, prefabricated dorm rooms. The scheme explored the intricate geometries available via individual, prefab furniture-like rooms to create a village plan within the enclosed space. The scheme addressed the interesting scenarios that could occur when weather protection became the job of the existing structure. We explored ventilation, building codes, and fabrication possibilities for this project.

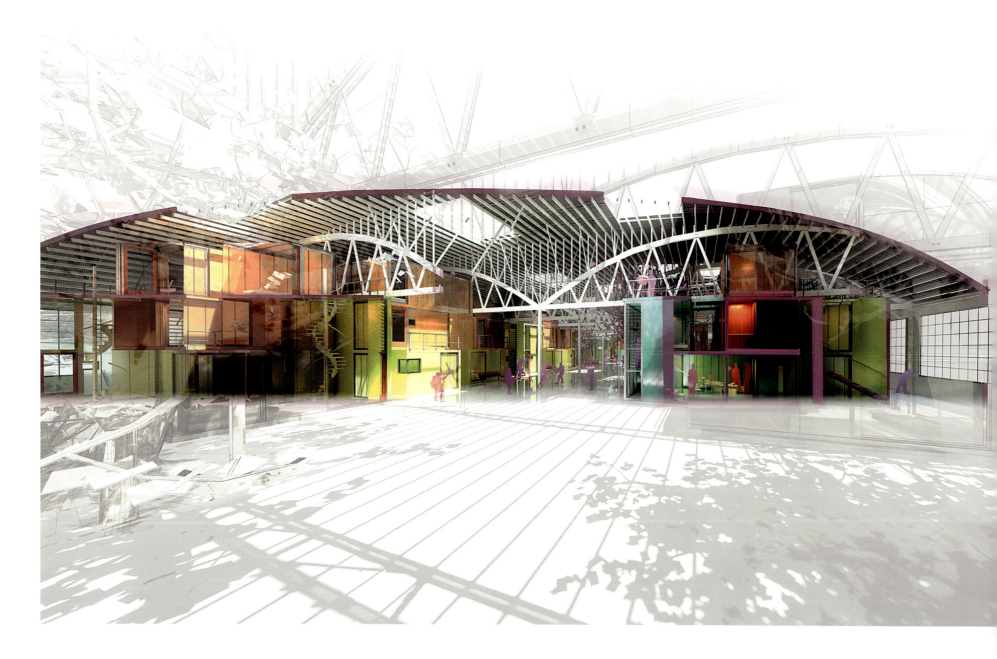

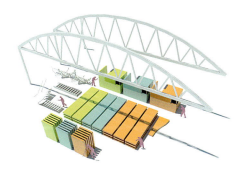

DELIVERY OF PREFABRICATED COMPONENTS
[SHEAR PANELS, FLOOR PLANKS, BATHROOM MODULES, STAIRS]

MODULE CONSTRUCTION
[ASSEMBLED COMPONENTS CREATE STRUCTURALLY INDEPENDENT MODULES]

COMPLETED UNITS
[SKINNING STRUCTURAL FRAME COMPLETES ASSEMBLY]

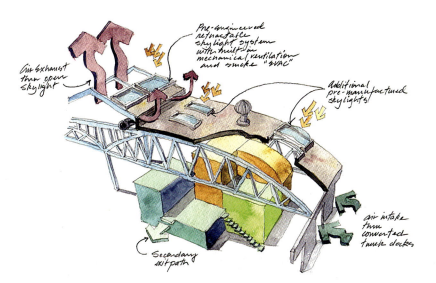

EDITING OF HISTORIC STRUCTURE
[CODE COMPLIANCE FOR HOUSING]

CENTRAL CALIFORNIA HISTORY MUSEUM

This was a design competition and exhibit for a new Central California History Museum to be located in Fresno. Our scheme created a high-energy architectural vernacular using symbols and imagery from California's agricultural heritage.

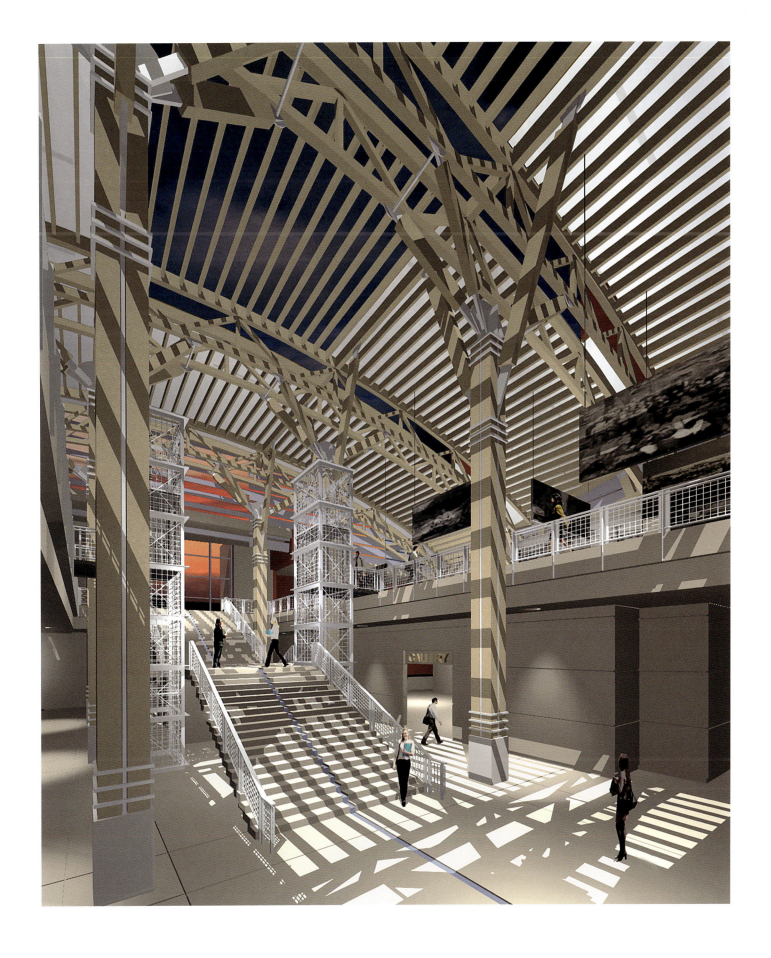

GRAND AVENUE DEVELOPMENT

This is our competition scheme to develop the parcel adjacent to Disney Concert Hall in downtown Los Angeles. It strengthened connectivity with County Court facilities and the Civic Center Mall (now Grand Park), running from City Hall to the Department of Water and Power. It also provided needed housing to further enhance the Bunker Hill development.

TOWERS

214

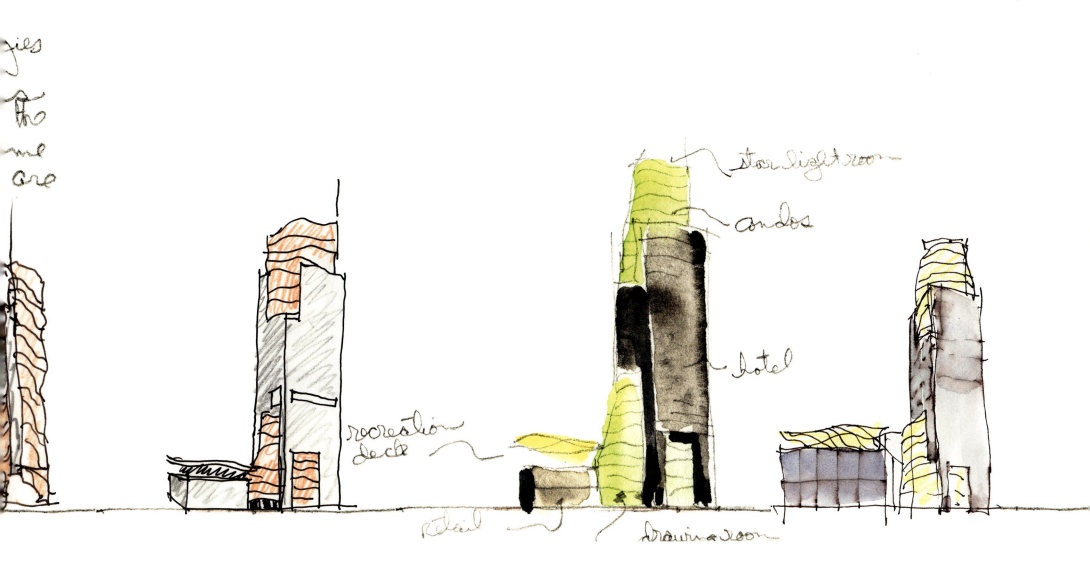

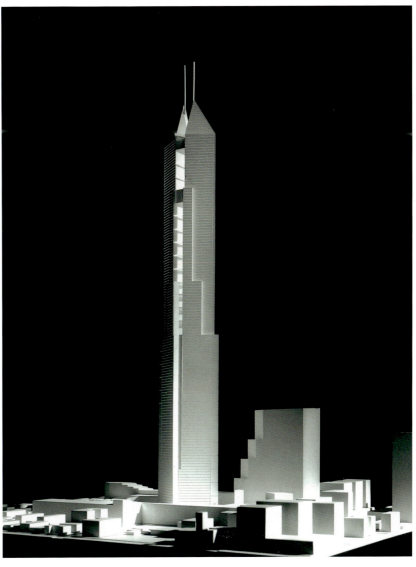

FURN
DES

TURE
SIGN

FURNITURE DESIGN

Furniture design involves form, function, style, economy, cost, craft, and trial and error. One might say it is the scale model of the architecture process. Furniture design for an architect is like short story writing for an author. Architecture has cycles or rhythms that start with inspiration and end with completion. It generally takes five years, often longer and rarely less, to design and construct a building; to make a film, maybe one year; a fashion line, five times a year. What is terrific about furniture design and fabrication is that it can be as rapid-fire as fashion, which for an architect used to long-term creative commitments, is truly a wonderful experience.

My interest in furniture design stems from this phenomenon, plus a few other idiosyncratic traits. I love to make things, and whether through naïveté, pure passion, or material desire, I have been making things all my life.

Two influences took this idea of creation to new levels. One was meeting Andrée Putman, who unfolded for Mary and me the furniture and design world of Chareau, Prouvé, Perriand, Gray, and many more. The other was possession of a metalworking machine shop that I had assembled to build and restore cars and motorcycles. It was relatively easy to make the leap from the world of engines and wheels to furniture fabrication. I would see a masterful Chareau table crafted by extraordinary blacksmith technology, go into my shop, and give it a try.

Actually, Robert Timme, former Dean of the USC School of Architecture, saw what I was doing with furniture in my shop and asked if I would start a furniture design and fabrication class at the school. We both felt that this type of hands-on experience was important yet seriously lacking for students of architecture, so I accepted the challenge and led the course for many years.

Design comes easily, but the craft of working with my hands is more difficult. The journey to that fine point where design, feedback, spontaneity, and master craftsmanship meet is as elusive as it is seductive. As Gordon Bunshaft said about designing glass buildings, "I'm going to keep doing it until I get it right."

Along with the joy of craft comes the appreciation of those masters who have gone before. To read about the life of Eileen Gray, to visit the Maison de Verre, to study the sketches of Prouvé—all bring me excitement and inspiration.

The following are some favorite pieces of mine. Some were done independently, while others were addressed by a team of creative people joining me in the process.

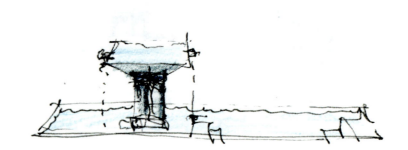

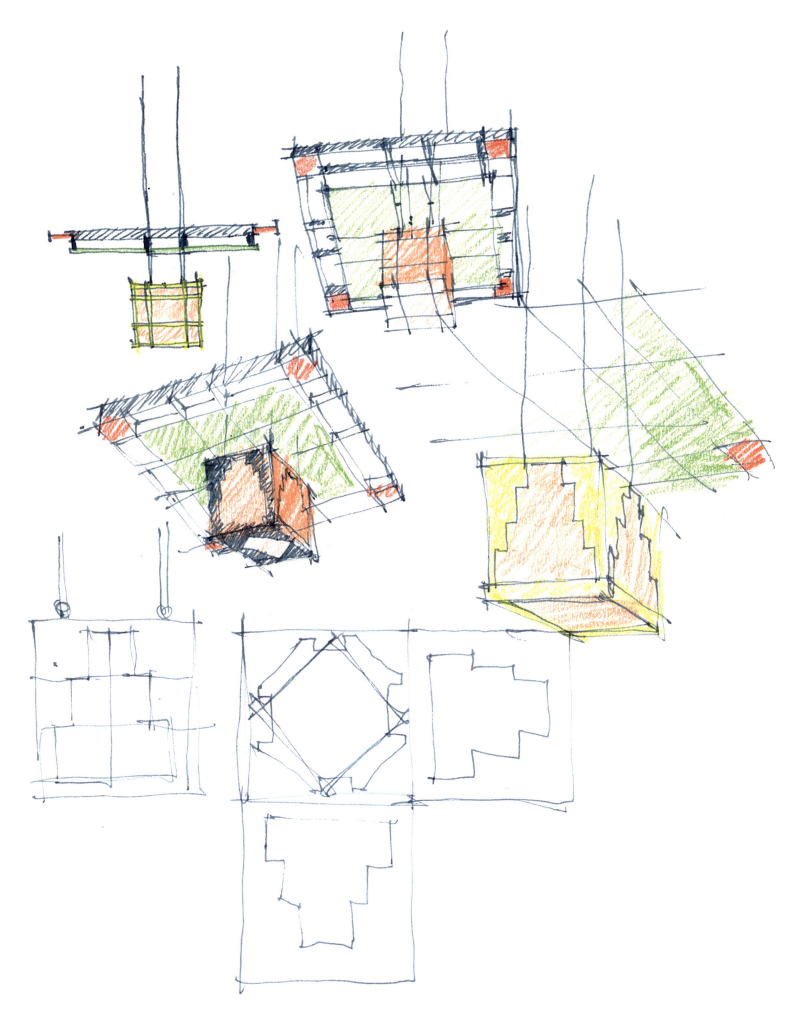

TREE TABLE

We have had a sustainable tree farm in the family for several generations. The table top shown came from a damaged tree, struck by lightning. We cut the tree trunk with a chainsaw rig and produced several large slabs. These slabs eventually became six pieces of furniture. This particular table was a gift to California State University, Fresno.

It is a simple idea of nature juxtaposed with technology. The base was created by a computer-generated form·Z drawing, where we stretched points, unfolded planes, and then created a file that was transferred to a fabrication shop.

Although the process seems simple enough, it involved the creation of some 30 options and several maquettes. An engineering analysis was done to ensure the stability of the amorphic base. The base traveled to a 100-year-old woodworking shop in Fresno, where the slab was planed, shaped, and joined to the base. The entire process was a reminder that everything we make in life is either grown or mined from the earth. Here we combined both in a simple way.

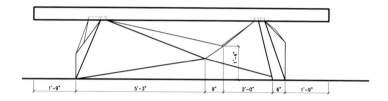

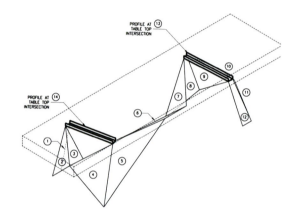

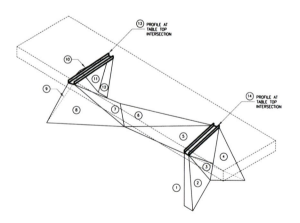

Z LAMP

The design of this light fixture deals with three simple ideas: 1) the creation of a warm, soft glow of light, like a single candle in a dark cathedral; 2) experimentation with resin to produce different shades of amber, depending on the thickness of resin in the lens; and 3) exploration of the plastic character of metal when heated to an almost fluid state. These ideas, with the juxtaposition of rigid geometries (rods, screws, amp, and bulb) against the flow of resin and bent steel, form the essence of this piece.

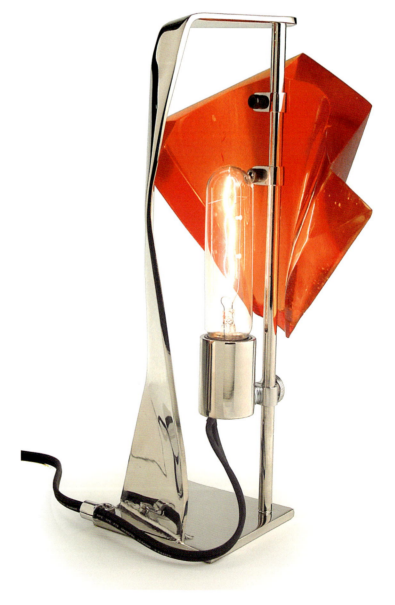

ALTAR CHAIRS

I had the opportunity to design a chapel for all faiths at Chapman University. Altogether, we involved five major artists for the art and architecture program.

These chairs were a collaboration between myself and artist William Tunberg, who created the exquisite marquetry panels. We worked back and forth on such small details as the curve of the panels and ergonomics of height and width.

The images that Bill created were inspired by images from the Hubbell Space Telescope. The chairs have become a successful part of the many rituals that exist when several religious denominations share the same space.

RUSTIC CANYON CHANDELIER

After ten years of living in our Rustic Canyon house, we finally acquired a grand dining table. Our space is tall, and we wanted the chandelier to not only add formality to the dining experience but also provide spatial connection between the table and the larger room.

This called for about 20 feet of cable, rigging, and armature. The individual lanterns are comprised of double cylinders of hand-blown glass by artist Kent Kahlen. The outer layer is clear to pick up reflections, while the inner layer is wine-colored to add effect to the incandescent filaments within the light bulbs.

These pieces, more than any other, required an intense collaboration to meet our schedule. The glassblower's challenge was to create the double walls of glass with some precision, the electrical design was integral to the steel fabrication, and the installation was as challenging as all other activities.

Unseen in the photos are a series of seismic restraints to protect the pieces in the event of an earthquake.

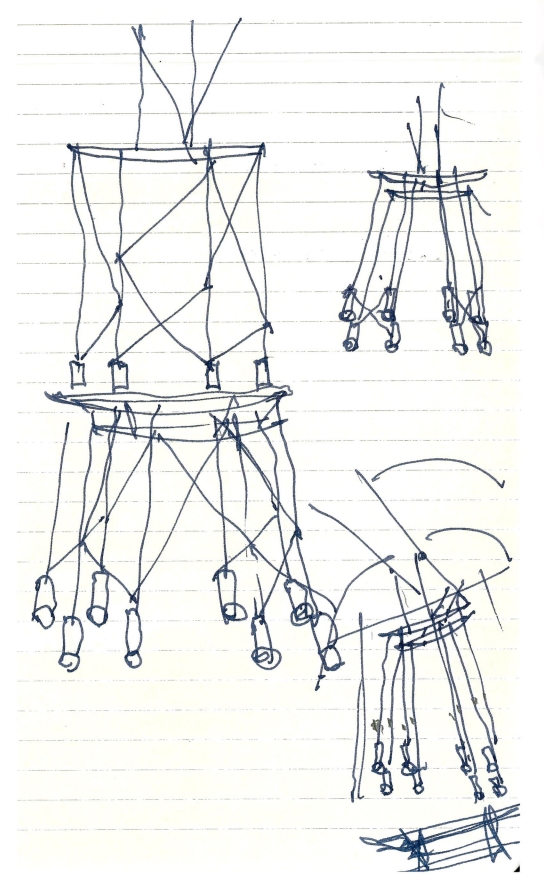

HIGH RISE TABLE

This side table was inspired by the motif of the 50-story Figueroa at Wilshire Tower that I designed for the Mitsui Fudosan Group and Gerald Hines Partners. The geometry of the entire architectural project, from the site plan down to the carpets, was a rigor of squares, rectangles, and diagonals. The table is comprised of sandblasted glass atop a lacquered bronze base and is an abstraction of the composition of the building.

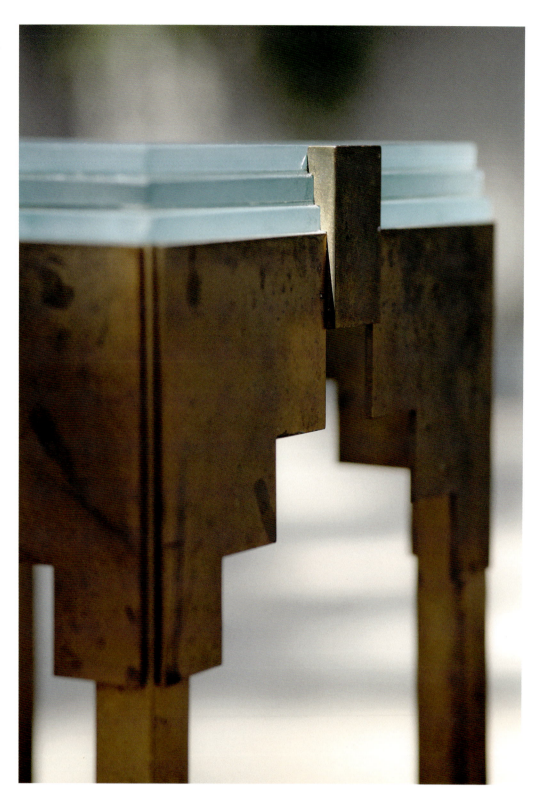

MUSIC DESK

Keyboards come in standard sizes and shapes and have a theoretical life, like many electronic devices, of about two years. This desk gives some sense of permanence as the keyboards are traded-out over the years. It is made of makore pommele and ebony veneer. The black aluminum cabinet houses effects and music-oriented computers. The studio is in constant technological flux, yet it has maintained a consistent look through the years.

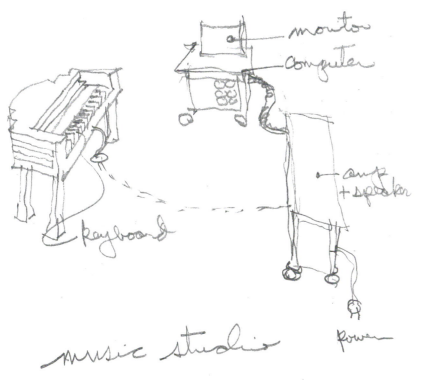

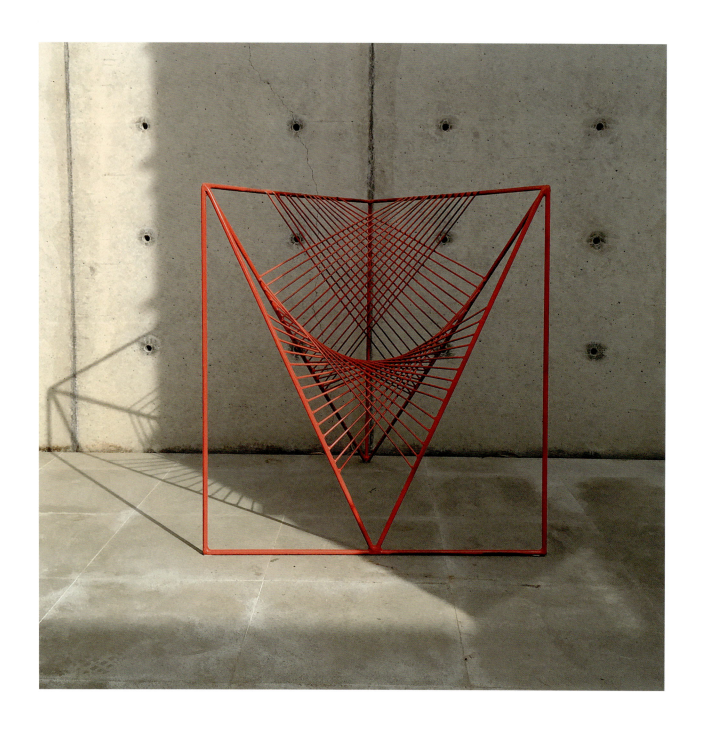

ARCH 481

The idea behind USC's ARCH 481 class is manyfold. It is primarily about the design and fabrication of small-scale furniture, but also provides architectural students with a literal hands-on experience with the nature of the materials, their characteristics, the tools of fabrication, and the limits thereof.

The premise of the class is quite simple, and the class is popular within the architectural curriculum. The appeal, in a way, is similar to the biggest challenge. The students come with a sophisticated sense of design, yet they represent a generation of young people who have not had the opportunity to use tools, to build, or to fix. Unlike my generation, everything around them is virtual, disposable, or too technical to mess with. Here, they are given the opportunity of their own volition to take an idea in their mind and bring it to full physical reality.

It is also a wonderful lesson in craft—to analyze a design, understand the materials of the concept, and the tools and hand manipulation required to achieve success. All this, done right, gives an immense sense of satisfaction that is at the root of making things well.

PRO.
CHRON

JECT-
OLOGY

1971

Sears, Roebuck and Company

Pacific Coast Territory

Administrative Offices

and Department Store

Alhambra, CA

1973

Beacon Bay Enterprises, Inc.

Beacon Bay Office Building

(Includes 5th Floor Residential Space)

Newport Beach, CA

1967

Columbia University Graduate School

of Architecture, Planning and Preservation (GSAPP)

Student Work – Roosevelt Island Development Plan

New York, NY

1972

Parker-Hannifin Aerospace

Engineering and Manufacturing Headquarters

Irvine, CA

1979

Hydril Company World Headquarters
Office and Manufacturing Facility
for Oil and Petroleum Exploration

Houston, TX

1981

Prudential Insurance Company
Western Home Office Headquarters

Westlake Village, CA

1980

IBM
Development and Manufacturing Facility

Tucson, AZ

1982

City of Thousand Oaks
Thousand Oaks Public Library

Thousand Oaks, CA

1984

Loyola Marymount University

Burns Fine Arts Center

Los Angeles, CA

1990

Mitsui Fudosan/Gerald Hines Partners

Sanwa Bank Plaza Office Building

and Ground-Level Retail

(Figueroa at Wilshire)

601 S. Figueroa Street, Los Angeles, CA

1983

Rockefeller Realty Corporation

Los Angeles Headquarters Office Building

and Retail Complex (Citigroup Center)

444 S. Flower Street, Los Angeles, CA

1985

Brin-Mar I

Towers at Brinderson Plaza

(Two Office Buildings)

Newport Beach, CA

1993

San Joaquin County Human Services Agency

Administrative Offices and Community Clinic

Stockton, CA

1995

Archdiocese of Los Angeles

Padre Serra Parish

Camarillo, CA

1999

University of California, Irvine

Humanities Instructional Building,

Music and Media Building,

and Fine Arts Building

Irvine, CA

1999

University of Southern California Popovich
Hall - Marshall Graduate School of Business

Los Angeles, CA

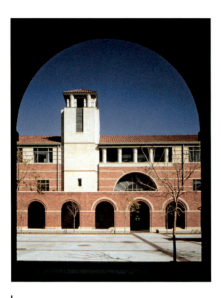

2000

Flintridge Preparatory School
Randall Performing Arts Center

La Cañada Flintridge, CA

2000

Archdiocese of Los Angeles
St. Maximilian Kolbe Catholic Church

Westlake Village, CA

2000

City of Sacramento/Thomas Properties
Group, LLC (Public/Private Partnership)
CalEPA Headquarters

Sacramento, CA

2001

City of Los Angeles

Los Angeles City Hall

Renovation and Seismic Upgrade

Los Angeles, CA

2002

California State University, Long Beach

Molecular & Life Sciences Center

Long Beach, CA

2002

Springleaf Tower

Singapore

2004

University of Southern California

Viterbi School of Engineering

Los Angeles, CA

2004

Chapman University

The Fish Interfaith Center

Orange, CA

2007
Judicial Council of California
Fifth District Court of Appeal
Fresno, CA

2009
City of Los Angeles
Hollenbeck Community Police Station
Boyle Heights, CA

2006
University of California, Davis
Mathematical Sciences Building
Davis, CA

2009
California State University, Fresno
Fresno State Library
Fresno, CA

2009
California Department of Transportation
Caltrans District 3 Headquarters
Marysville, CA

2012

Roman Catholic Diocese of Orange County

Our Lady Queen of Angels Catholic Church

Newport Beach, CA

2015

Judicial Council of California

Superior Court of California, County of Madera

Madera, CA

2010

University of Southern California

Ronald Tutor Campus Center

Los Angeles, CA

2017

Korean Air

Wilshire Grand Center Hotel,

Restaurant, and Office Complex

900 Wilshire Boulevard, Los Angeles, CA

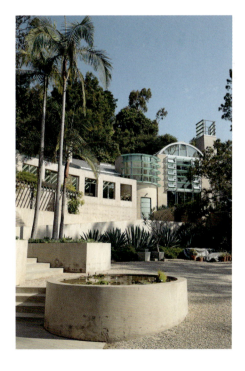

1994 – PRESENT

David C. Martin and Mary Klaus Martin

Rustic Canyon Residence

Santa Monica, CA

ACKNOWLEDGMENTS

CHRISTOPHER C. MARTIN

My cousin, Chris, never doubted that we could live up to the expectations of our fathers and carry AC Martin into a third generation.

Chris became associated with the firm as a college student, as did I. It was 1970, and I was already on board. More than a decade passed before we assumed leadership roles. Chris became managing partner in 1986, when the firm was 80 years old, and later served as chairman and CEO through 2019. Tom Hsieh succeeded Chris as CEO, and Chris continues as chairman.

Did we always get along? Chris told the Los Angeles Times in 1998: "The firm was big enough that we could each do our own thing. David had his projects, and I had mine." This is true, though he recently said, "We had differences of opinion about strategies and budget, but it was never personal. We were not competitive in any way. We knew that when we worked together, we got a better product."

We agreed that the family's legacy was the priority. We were Martins, and we understood the responsibility that came along with the name. We considered it a shared responsibility.

During our early years with the firm, our fathers provided us with sound advice. They once told Chris, "We have always had an inside guy and an outside guy. Your mission is to be the outside guy and get involved with civic organizations." Chris had no fear. His role entailed spreading the word that AC Martin had the talent to design buildings of substance and integrity. In the days before we had portable computers, he often brought along a scale model of L.A.'s government center when meeting with Mayor Bradley or other public leaders. He was deeply involved in the Central City Association, and his activities with that organization greatly benefited the firm.

When the recession in the late 1980's hit our practice, Chris was the one who saw us through it. As markets were drying up and clients were declaring bankruptcy, we found ourselves occupying six floors of the Fine Arts Building with staff scattered throughout. Affording the rent was a concern. Chris sought advice from his father, who said, "Don't spend money on rent you can't afford. And don't think it is your fault. It is force majeure. Talk it over with the accountants." His solution was to consolidate our practice onto three floors.

In the late 1990's, resulting from Chris's leadership in the community, AC Martin was selected to upgrade Los Angeles City Hall with a $273 million seismic rehabilitation. Having designed the facility in 1928, the firm was honored to have the opportunity to revisit the structure and strengthen it against future earthquake damage. All four generations of the family worked on City Hall, including Chris's son, Patrick, who passed away in 2012.

The culmination of our business relationship was the Wilshire Grand Center, a dream project for our firm. As Chris recounts it, "Wilshire Grand was a godsend, allowing me and David to collaborate on an extraordinary project at the end of our careers. What a joy and pleasure for both of us, courtesy of Chairman Cho of Korean Air, one of the best clients the firm has ever had. For some reason, he had a lot of personal trust in me, and he liked David."

Our partnership lasted 45 years.

AC MARTIN STAFF AND CLIENTS

Architecture is a high-drama profession. It usually pits creativity against time and money. It is also a slow process. It takes one or two years to design a building. That, coupled with the number of people involved, makes relationships and camaraderie important. When it's right, it's a very exciting game.

Over my years at AC Martin, I was fortunate to work with the most talented, interesting people imaginable. Continually working together, teams often become quite efficient. You know each other's strengths and weaknesses, and you know how to get things done in exciting and enjoyable ways. It's a big part of the creative architectural process.

I'll never forget the studio culture involving Ron Pagliassotti, Roy Tanaka, and Ed Abrahamian. I was just out of school, and these guys were determined to make me succeed. Then we were joined by Dave Larson and my good friend, the talented Michael O'Sullivan. A decade later, Gene McLean was the true talent in the Orange County office. Also from that office was Ken Lewis (who later became president of the company), Jon Starr, and John Johnson.

In these early years, our general manager was the extraordinary Robert Braunschweiger. He was not only an exceptional GM, but had the skills to deal with the unique characteristics of each of the four partners. For about five years, we had the amazing Tim Vreeland, who not only did fabulous work, but taught us all the significance of a strong historical perspective. Craig Webb was around at this time and went on to be a major player in Frank Gehry's office. Then we were joined by Gail Bouvrie. Gail, like myself, grew up in an architectural family. Her constant sense of professionalism was an inspiration to us all. Her presence added to our legacy. Tammy Jow joined us, and to this day, she drives everyone around her to excel. Paul Coleman and I worked on a number of projects, and his designs represent some of our best work. Jeff Su, with his incredible 3D modeling skills, helped us visualize every project. Richard Thompson ran our planning department, and we went through a lot of adventures together. Before Richard, Don Brackenbush was the planning director. He and I traveled the world in our planning pursuits. John Uniack came out of the planning group and came with me when I moved on to establish the MADWORKSHOP Foundation. Dick Tipping, Truls Ovrum, Robert Wilkerson, Gus Ullner, Don Toy, Richard Halfon, and Len Marvin were also great collaborators. Aram Tatikian was our production leader, always a key position concerning the quality and longevity of our buildings.

And I collaborated with many very talented young professionals, including Patrick Martin, Yogesh Seth, Jamie Myer, Sandra Lévesque, Eun Gu Lee, Rana Makaram, and Daniel Shirk.

Carey McLeod and Bob Murrin were great project managers, both as team leaders and as firm ambassadors. Oliver Santos was the firm's accountant, but most importantly, he watched over the family in a very protective way. Joanne Camacho was another professional that I both admired and enjoyed working with. We shared a keen interest in art and graphics. Jean Lloyd was a personnel director who had the right people skills to get things done "right now" at all levels of our endeavors. The Wilshire Grand project was in the office for almost ten years, and we had a dedicated team including "the young Turks"—recent graduates Joe Varholick of Cal Poly San Luis Obispo, Isaac Luna of USC, and Noel Moreno of Harvard University—all of whom helped expedite the team's understanding of parametric modeling, and Danielle Martin-Spicer, George vanGilluwe, Grit Pasker, Onik Tahtakran, and the fabulous Dr. Susan Painter.

Several professionals moved on from our firm to establish successful practices of their own. Although we always missed them, we were proud to witness their entrepreneurial accomplishments. These included many luminaries such as Carl McLarand, Ron Pagliassotti, Roy Tanaka, Ed Abrahamian, Fred Fisher, Mark Lee, Ron Frink, Nabih Youssef, and Chris King.

On the client side, there were a number who truly championed the architectural process. During the first part of my career, I worked primarily for real estate developers, and I would like to call out a few organizations. I found Gerald Hines Partners to be very supportive of good practices and sensitive to the value of design, and also, the partnership of Maguire Thomas, with Jim Thomas, the dynamic and often surprising Rob Maguire, Nelson Rising, and Ned Fox.

We did great work with the Mitsui Fudosan Group on Sanwa Bank Plaza (Figueroa at Wilshire) and with the entire Cho Family on Wilshire Grand Center. Heather Cho and her father were dynamic, to say the least, and always demanding, but in a good way. My experience with the LAPD and the members of the Hollenbeck Community Police Station was also very special. I developed a strong respect for law enforcement professionals, and I truly admire their community work.

The courthouse was a favorite building type of mine. Working with the state and federal judges was always a treat. Another special building type was the house of worship. I had the honor of working with Father Liam Kidney and a spirited group of dedicated Catholic priests. The first thing you learn is that they are human, but with a special mission to help people.

Working with two state agencies, in particular, enriched my life. One was CalEPA. Together, we created a headquarters building that was perhaps the best-performing structure in the country for about a ten-year period. The other was Caltrans, a wonderful organization where esprit de corps is palpable. For its Northern California headquarters, we explored a group of space-planning strategies that fostered collegiality.

Finally, I want to mention Chapman University in Orange, California. We worked for years with a wonderful group of people there, including President James Doti, a terrific leader, and Kris Olsen, Vice President of Campus Planning and Operations, an interesting and respected professional.

CREDITS

CONTRIBUTORS TO *LEGACY*

From my first thought of documenting my career at AC Martin, my dear friend, Edie Cohen, set to work as writer, editor, and project director of *Legacy*. I can't thank her enough for taking on the project with such enthusiasm.

Nhan-Nhi Lillian Nguyen, a MADWORKSHOP fellow, also supported *Legacy* from the outset, gathering imagery from AC Martin's archives and establishing a graphic design direction for the book.

Jennifer Duclett, a former staff member at AC Martin, provided copy editing and proofreading, and interfaced with ORO Editions during the critical, final phases of the effort.

I appreciate all of their hard work to bring *Legacy* to fruition.

PHOTOGRAPHERS

I am grateful to each of the following photographers for capturing the essence of our work so well: Joe Aker, Tom Bonner, Matt Cobleigh, James Ewing, Art Gray, Tim Griffith, Timothy Hursley, Eric Laignel, Jack Laxer, Gary Leonard, Mark Lohman, Susan Narduli, David Oakley, Marvin Rand, Julius Shulman, Tim Street-Porter, Wayne Thom, and John Uniack.

ORO Editions
Publishers of Architecture, Art, and Design
Gordon Goff: Publisher

www.oroeditions.com
info@oroeditions.com

Published by ORO Editions

Copyright © 2024 MADWORKSHOP

All rights reserved. No part of this book may be reproduced, stored in a retrieval system, or transmitted in any form or by any means, including electronic, mechanical, photocopying of microfilming, recording, or otherwise (except that copying permitted by Sections 107 and 108 of the US Copyright Law and except by reviewers for the public press) without written permission from the publisher.

You must not circulate this book in any other binding or cover and you must impose this same condition on any acquirer.

Author: David C. Martin
Introductory Essay and Interview: Edie Cohen
Book Design: Pablo Mandel / CircularStudio
Project Manager: Jake Anderson

10 9 8 7 6 5 4 3 2 1 First Edition

ISBN: 978-1-957183-58-9

Prepress and Print work by ORO Editions Inc.
Printed in China

ORO Editions makes a continuous effort to minimize the overall carbon footprint of its publications. As part of this goal, ORO, in association with Global ReLeaf, arranges to plant trees to replace those used in the manufacturing of the paper produced for its books. Global ReLeaf is an international campaign run by American Forests, one of the world's oldest nonprofit conservation organizations. Global ReLeaf is American Forests' education and action program that helps individuals, organizations, agencies, and corporations improve the local and global environment by planting and caring for trees.